First World War
and Army of Occupation
War Diary
France, Belgium and Germany

42 DIVISION
Headquarters, Branches and Services
Commander Royal Engineers
1 March 1917 - 31 March 1919

WO95/2648/2

The Naval & Military Press Ltd
www.nmarchive.com
Published in association with The National Archives

Published by

The Naval & Military Press Ltd

Unit 10 Ridgewood Industrial Park,

Uckfield, East Sussex,

TN22 5QE England

Tel: +44 (0) 1825 749494

www.naval-military-press.com

www.nmarchive.com

This diary has been reprinted in facsimile from the original. Any imperfections are inevitably reproduced and the quality may fall short of modern type and cartographic standards.

© Crown Copyright
Images reproduced by permission of The National Archives, London, England, 2015.

Contents

Document type	Place/Title	Date From	Date To
Heading	WO95/2648/2		
Heading	C.R.E. Mar 1917-Mar 1919		
Heading	War Diary Of Headquarters. 42nd (East Lancs) Div. R.E. from 1st to 31st March. 1917 (Volume 4)		
War Diary	At Sea.	01/03/1917	01/03/1917
War Diary	Marseilles	02/03/1917	04/03/1917
War Diary	Pont Remy	05/03/1917	05/03/1917
War Diary	Hocquincourt	06/03/1917	28/03/1917
War Diary	Herbecourt	29/03/1917	31/03/1917
Heading	War Diary of H.Q. R.E. 42nd Div. from 1st to 30th April (Volume 4)		
War Diary	Herbecourt	01/04/1917	01/04/1917
War Diary	Peronne	06/04/1917	30/04/1917
Heading	War Diary Of Headquarters R.E. 42nd (East Lancs) Division. from 1st to 31st May. 1917 (Volume 4)		
War Diary	Peronne	01/05/1917	03/05/1917
War Diary	K.11.a.99.	04/05/1917	19/05/1917
War Diary	Brusle	20/05/1917	23/05/1917
War Diary	Ytres	23/05/1917	31/05/1917
Heading	War Diary of H.Q. R.E. 42nd (E. Lancs) Div. from 1st to 30th June 1917 (Volume 4)		
War Diary	Little Wood Ytres	01/06/1917	15/06/1917
War Diary	Ytres	16/06/1917	30/06/1917
Operation(al) Order(s)	42nd Division Order No. 22. Appendix A	26/05/1917	26/05/1917
Miscellaneous	Chief Engineer, III Corps. Appendix B	26/06/1917	26/06/1917
Miscellaneous	To C.R.E., 42nd Division. From O.C., 427 Field Co. R.E.	24/06/1917	24/06/1917
Miscellaneous Map	Table Of Tools & Stores.	06/06/1917	06/06/1917
Operation(al) Order(s)	C.R.E., 42nd (E. Lancs.) Division, Order No. 1.	19/06/1917	19/06/1917
Operation(al) Order(s)	C.R.E., 42nd (E. Lancs.) Division, Order No. 2	27/06/1917	27/06/1917
Heading	War Diary Of H.Q. R.E. 42nd (E.L.) Div. from 1st to 31st July 1917. (Volume 4)		
War Diary	Ytres	01/07/1917	09/07/1917
War Diary	Achiet Le Petit	10/07/1917	31/07/1917
Miscellaneous	O.C., 427, 428, 429 Field Co. R.E. Appendix A	10/07/1917	10/07/1917
Miscellaneous	O.C., 427, 428, 429 Field Co. R.E. Appendix A		
Miscellaneous	Appendix A.	31/07/1917	31/07/1917
Miscellaneous	O.C. 429 Field Co. R.E. Appendix B	20/07/1917	20/07/1917
Miscellaneous	Scheme for Training in Bridging For 429 Field Company R.E. Appendix B		
Miscellaneous	O.C. 427 Field Co. R.E. Appendix C	23/07/1917	23/07/1917
Miscellaneous	Scheme For Training In Bridging For 427 Field Co. R.E. Appendix C	23/07/1917	23/07/1917
Miscellaneous	O.C., 428 Field Co. R.E. Appendix D	23/07/1917	23/07/1917
Miscellaneous	Scheme For Training In Causeway And Bridging Work For 428 Field Co. R.E. Appendix D	23/07/1917	23/07/1917
Heading	War Diary Of H.Q. R.E. 42nd (E. Lancs) Div. T.F. from 1st to 31st August 1917 Volume 4		
War Diary	Achiet Le Petit	01/08/1917	20/08/1917

War Diary	Acheux Aveluy	21/08/1917	23/08/1917
War Diary	Watou	24/08/1917	31/08/1917
Heading	War Diary Of H.Q. R.E. 42 (E.Z.) Div from 1st to 30th Sept 1917 Volume 4		
War Diary	Bran	01/09/1917	17/09/1917
War Diary	Poperinghe	18/09/1917	21/09/1917
War Diary	La Panne	22/09/1917	24/09/1917
War Diary	St Idesbald	25/09/1917	30/09/1917
Miscellaneous	Report On R.E. Work Carried Out In Connection With Operations Against Iberian Beck House And Berry Farm. App A		
Miscellaneous	C.R.E., 42nd (E. Lancs) Division Order No. 16	13/09/1917	13/09/1917
Operation(al) Order(s)	C.R.E., 42nd (E. Lancs) Division Order No. 17	16/09/1917	16/09/1917
Operation(al) Order(s)	C.R.E., 42nd (E. Lancs) Division Order No. 19	19/09/1917	19/09/1917
Operation(al) Order(s)	C.R.E., 42nd (E. Lancs) Division Order No. 20	20/09/1917	20/09/1917
Miscellaneous	Addendum No. 1 to C.R.E., Operation Order No. 20 by Lt Colonel D.S. Macinnes, C.M.G., D.S.O., R.E.	05/10/1917	05/10/1917
Operation(al) Order(s)	C.R.E., 42nd (E. Lancs) Division Operation Order No. 20 by Lieut Colonel D.S. Macinnes, C.M.G., D.S.O., R.E.	04/10/1917	04/10/1917
Miscellaneous	Location Of Field Coys. R.E. 42nd Division.		
Heading	War Diary Of H.Q.R.E. 42nd (E.L.) Division from 1st To 31st October 1917 Volume 4		
War Diary	St. Idesbald	01/10/1917	07/10/1917
War Diary	Coxyde Bains	08/10/1917	31/10/1917
Heading	War Diary Of H.Q. R.E. 42nd (E.L.) Division from 1st To 30th November 1917 Volume 4		
War Diary	Coxyde Bains	01/11/1917	18/11/1917
War Diary	Wormhoudt	19/11/1917	19/11/1917
War Diary	Aire	20/11/1917	30/11/1917
War Diary	Locon		
Miscellaneous	Report On Dam 66 App A	04/11/1917	04/11/1917
Miscellaneous	C.R.E., 42nd (East. Lancs) Division (Warning) Order No. 28 App B	14/11/1917	14/11/1917
Operation(al) Order(s)	C.R.E., 42nd (East. Lancs) Division Order No. 29 App C	15/11/1917	15/11/1917
Miscellaneous	March Table to Accompany C.R.E., 42nd Division Order No. 29		
Miscellaneous	Working Party Table to Accompany C.R.E. 42nd Division Order No. 29		
Operation(al) Order(s)	C.R.E. 42nd (E. Lancs) Division Order No. 30 by Lt. Colonel A. N. Lawford. R.E. App D	25/11/1917	25/11/1917
Miscellaneous	March Table For 42nd Divisional R.E.		
Miscellaneous	O.C. 427 Field Co. R.E. App E	25/11/1917	25/11/1917
Heading	War Diary of Hdqrs R.E. 42nd (E.L.) Division from 1st to 31st December, 1917 Volume 4		
War Diary	Locon	01/12/1917	31/12/1917
Miscellaneous	D.A.G. 3rd Echelon, B.E.F.	10/04/1917	10/04/1917
Heading	War Diary Of Hdqrs R.E. 42nd (E. Lancs) Division from 1st to 31st January 1918 Volume 5		
War Diary	Locon	01/01/1918	31/01/1918
Heading	War Diary Of Hdqrs R.E. 42nd (E. Lancs) Division R.E. from 1st to 28th February 1918 Volume 5		
War Diary	Locon	01/02/1918	15/02/1918
War Diary	Hinges	16/02/1918	28/02/1918

Type	Description	From	To
Operation(al) Order(s)	C.R.E., 42nd (East. Lancs) Division Order No. 34 by Lieut Colonel R.E.B. Pratt, D.S.O., R.E. App A	10/02/1918	10/02/1918
Miscellaneous	March Table to Accompany C.R.E.'s Order No. 34		
Heading	C.R.E. 42nd East Lancs Division March 1918		
Heading	War Diary Of Hdqrs R.E. 42nd (E.L.) Division from 1st to 31st March 1918 Volume 5		
War Diary	Hinges	01/03/1918	05/03/1918
War Diary	La Beuvriere	06/03/1918	23/03/1918
War Diary	Adinfer	24/03/1918	24/03/1918
War Diary	Monchy au Bois	25/03/1918	25/03/1918
War Diary	Fonquevillers	26/03/1918	28/03/1918
War Diary	St Amand	29/03/1918	31/03/1918
Heading	Headquarters, Royal Engineers, 42nd Division. April 1918		
Heading	War Diary Headquarters 42nd Division RE from 1st to 30th April 1918		
War Diary	St Amand	01/04/1918	03/04/1918
War Diary	Henu	04/04/1918	07/04/1918
War Diary	Pas	08/04/1918	16/04/1918
War Diary	Couin	17/04/1918	30/04/1918
Heading	H.Q. R.E. 42nd Division May 1918 Volume 4		
War Diary	Couin	01/05/1918	06/05/1918
War Diary	Pas	07/05/1918	31/05/1918
Heading	War Diary Of H.Q. R.E. 42nd Division from 1st June 1918 to 30th June 1918 Volume IV		
War Diary	Pas	01/06/1918	07/06/1918
War Diary	Bus-Les-Artois	08/06/1918	30/06/1918
Operation(al) Order(s)	C.R.E., 42nd (East. Lancs) Division Order No. 39 by Lieut. Colonel R.E.B. Pratt, D.S.O., R.E.	03/06/1918	03/06/1918
Miscellaneous	Table of Moves and Reliefs to Accompany C.R.E. 42nd Division, Order No. 39	03/06/1918	03/06/1918
Miscellaneous	Amendment No. 1 to C.R.E. 42nd Division Order No. 39	04/06/1918	04/06/1918
Operation(al) Order(s)	C.R.E., 42nd (East Lancs) Division Order No. 37 by Lieut. Colonel R.E.B. Pratt, D.S.O., R.E.	01/06/1918	01/06/1918
Operation(al) Order(s)	C.R.E., 42nd (East Lancs) Division Order No. 38 by Lieut. Colonel R.E.B. Pratt, D.S.O., R.E.	01/06/1918	01/06/1918
Heading	War Diary H.Q. R.E. 42nd Division Volume 4		
War Diary	Bus-Les-Artois	01/07/1918	18/07/1918
War Diary	Authie	16/07/1918	31/07/1918
Heading	War Diary Of Hd. Qrs. 42nd Divisional RE August 1918 Vol 4		
War Diary	Authie	01/08/1918	14/08/1918
War Diary	Bus-Les-Artois	15/08/1918	24/08/1918
War Diary	Colincamps	25/08/1918	26/08/1918
War Diary	Near Achiet-Le Petit	27/08/1918	29/08/1918
War Diary	Grevillers	30/08/1918	31/08/1918
Heading	War Diary Headquarters 42nd Divisional RE September 1st to 30th 1918 Vol 4		
Heading	War Diary September 1918		
War Diary	Grevillers	01/09/1918	20/09/1918
War Diary	Nuvelu	21/09/1918	30/09/1918
Miscellaneous	O.C. 427 Field Coy, R.E.	26/09/1918	26/09/1918
Heading	War Diary Headquarters 42nd Divisional RE October 1918		
War Diary	Velu	01/10/1918	08/10/1918

War Diary	Esnes	09/10/1918	11/10/1918
War Diary	Beauvois	12/10/1918	31/10/1918
Heading	War Diary November 1918 Volume IV		
War Diary	Hautmont	01/11/1918	04/11/1918
War Diary	Potelle	05/11/1918	07/11/1918
War Diary	Petit Bayay	08/11/1918	08/11/1918
War Diary	Hautmont	09/11/1918	30/11/1918
Heading	War Diary Of H.Q. 42nd Divnl RE for Month Of December 1918	04/01/1919	04/01/1919
War Diary	Hautmont	01/12/1918	12/12/1918
War Diary	Charleroi	13/12/1918	31/12/1918
Heading	War Diary H.Q. 42nd (E. Lancs) Division RE from Jan 1st to 31st 1919 Volume 6		
War Diary	Charleroi	01/01/1919	31/01/1919
Heading	42nd Division R.E. February 1919 Volume		
War Diary	Charleroi	01/02/1919	28/02/1919
Miscellaneous	Divisional H.Q.R.E. (Casualties)		
Heading	War Diary H.Q. R.E. 42nd Division from 1st to 31st March 1919 Volume 5		
War Diary	Charleroi	01/03/1919	31/03/1919

WO 95
2648/2

42ND DIVISION

C. R. E.
MAR 1917-MAR 1919

Vol 2

CONFIDENTIAL.

War Diary.

of

Headquarters. 42nd (East Lancs) Div: R.E.

from 1st to 31st March. 1917.

(Volume 4)

Army Form C. 2118

WAR DIARY
~~INTELLIGENCE SUMMARY~~
(Erase heading not required.)

Instructions regarding War Diaries and Intelligence Summaries are contained in F. S. Regs., Part II. and the Staff Manual respectively. Title Pages will be prepared in manuscript.

Place	Date	Hour	Summary of Events and Information	Remarks and references to Appendices
At Sea.	Mar. 1st.		H.Q. R.E. at sea in transit from ALEXANDRIA to MARSEILLES.	
MARSEILLES.	2nd		Disembarked at MARSEILLES. Entrained for Divisional Area.	
	3, 4		In Train.	
PONT REMY.	5		Detrained at PONT REMY. Proceeded to HOCQUINCOURT (3 miles) and billetted.	
HOCQUINCOURT	6-28		AT HOCQUINCOURT. Administered R.E. Services for 3 Brigades and Divisional Troops in the Back Area of the 4th Army allotted to 42nd Division. Principally putting into order and running Baths. (Each soldier got a 6-minute hot shower bath every 10 days or less). Minor R.E. Services also carried out.	
			427 Co. left area with its Brigade on the 15th, but the other 2 Companies were trained in Bridging and rapid wiring as practised at 4th Army School of Instruction. A great deal of lecturing on training and administration, as set forth in various official pamphlets was carried out.	
HERBECOURT.	29		H.Q.R.E. moved by motor lorry to HERBECOURT (4 miles W. of PERONNE) to superintend Road Repair in Corps Area West of River SOMME with 125 Brigade working parties.	
	30, 31		At HERBECOURT. Took over administration of roads from Corps Roads Officer.	

A. Mohunwalla.
Lieut. R.E.
Adjt. for Lt.-Col.
C.R.E. 42nd Division.

Vol 3

CONFIDENTIAL.

ORIGINAL

WAR DIARY
of
H.Q.R.E. 42nd Divn.
from 1st to 30th APRIL.

(Volume 4)

ORIGINAL.

WAR DIARY
or
INTELLIGENCE SUMMARY.
(Erase heading not required.)

Army Form C. 2118.

Place	Date	Hour	Summary of Events and Information	Remarks and references to Appendices
HERBECOURT.	April 1st		H.Q. R.E. with 2 sections 429 Fd C.R.E. supervising repair of road HERBECOURT – BIASHE – CHAPELETTE for motor transport (main artery for III Corps road traffic Eastwards)	
PERONNE	April 6th	16.30	H.Q. R.E. moved to PERONNE to supervise road repair as far East as line TEMPLEUX-LA-FOSSE to TINCOURT to ESTREES-EN-CHAUSSES, as well as bridges over SOMME and COLOGNE rivers in 42nd Divisional Area. Road metal very scarce till 16th when the railway into PERONNE having been completed, trains of metal came in at nearly one a day. Principal work was repairing craters blown up by retreating enemy, principally at cross roads. The ruined cottages in villages provided abundant brick for repairs which might not have been available had the enemy not destroyed them. 3 road rollers became available about April 23. (1 Company) 1 D.E. (say 428th) kept for Corps work throughout the month) Considerable work by the D.E. on repairing houses in PERONNE billets & searching for mines & wires which the enemy might have laid.	Thoroughly read CRE 9 2 Div

Vol 4

WAR DIARY
OF
Headquarters R.E.
42° (East Lancs) Division.

from 1st to 31st May. 1917

(Volume 4)

Confidential
Original

Army Form C. 2118.

Instructions regarding War Diaries and Intelligence Summaries are contained in F. S. Regs., Part II. and the Staff Manual respectively. Title pages will be prepared in manuscript.

WAR DIARY
INTELLIGENCE SUMMARY.
(Erase heading not required.)

Reference Maps: FRANCE Sheets 62c & 57c
Scale 1:40,000

Place	Date	Hour	Summary of Events and Information	Remarks and references to Appendices
PERONNE	1-5-17 to 2-5-17		The Field Companies moved up into forward area of Left Division of III Corps. One Field Company of the 48th Division rly was relieved, the other two Coys together with the 1/5 R. Sussex Pioneers remained in the area to assist in the proposed work.	MM
	3-5-17		H.Q.R.E. moved to 62c.K.11.a.99 and took over from C.R.E. 48th Division.	MM
K.11.a.99	4-5-17 to 11-5-17		A forward line of defence called the "Brown Line" running from 62c.F.29 central, North to 62c.F.12.c.09 and thence to 62c.X.13d.9.5., consisting of a number of posts with entrances wired in front, had been wired out and work was pushed on rapidly. The line was made ready for defence on May 6th but much additional work such as thickening wire and digging communication trenches was continued. Simultaneously work on the "Brown Line" of defence running along the forward slope of the ridge joining EPEHY and LEMPIRE, previously sited, was continued under the Field Company in reserve, which also maintained the water supply. The Pioneer Battalion assisted on roads in LEMPIRE and from ST EMILIE to RONSSOY were prepared as far as possible for motor lorries in accordance with III Corps instructions. The Brit. R.E. Dumps at ST EMILIE was considerably developed. Two sections of the 150th Tunnelling Coy R.E. were employed on developing wells in forward area.	MM
	12-5-17		The 474th, 477th Coys R.E. and 1/5 R. Sussex Pioneers returned to the 48th Division and 170 ay 2nd Co. 2nd R.E. was brought back into reserve.	MM
	13-5-17 (to 16-5-17)		Work continued as above. The taking over from 20th Division and handing over to 2nd & 3rd Cavalry Divisions commenced.	MM

Army Form C. 2118.

WAR DIARY
or
INTELLIGENCE SUMMARY.

(Erase heading not required.)

Reference Maps
FRANCE. Sheet 62c and 57c
Scale 1:40,000

Instructions regarding War Diaries and Intelligence Summaries are contained in F.S. Regs., Part II. and the Staff Manual respectively. Title pages will be prepared in manuscript.

Place	Date	Hour	Summary of Events and Information	Remarks and references to Appendices
KLA. 99	17-5-17 to 19-5-17		The Field Companies moved into the New Area, 57c P.2 and Q. On May 19th HQRE moved to BRUSLE	MM
BRUSLE	20-5-17 to 22-5-17		HQRE in MEERNE.	MM
	23-5-17		HQRE moved to "LITTLE WOOD" YPRES (57c P.26 central) and took over from CRE 20th Division.	MM
YPRES	23-5-17 to 31-5-17		The Field Companies together with the 256th Tunnelling Coy RE were engaged in Superintendence of front line defences, deep and splinter-proof dugouts, water and trails. Supply development and improvement of trails in the Nused village. A scheme for tunnel tramways was negotiated. The 2nd A.R.E. Branch was opened at RUYAUCOURT and material buy-dump.	MM
			Casualties.	
	7-5-17		Lieut F.H. STOREY, R.A.M.C. to hospital	
	20-5-17		Lieut Col. E.N. MOZLEY, D.S.O., R.E. to hospital. Major G.G. RIDDICK, O.C. 429 Fd Cy R.E. took over duties of A/CRE.	

A. Melman Walker
Lieut (Acting)
Major for CRE
MD Div

Confidential

ORIGINAL

WAR DIARY.

of

H.Q.R.E
42nd (E. Lancs) Div⁴

from 1st to 30th June 1917.

(Volume 4)

WAR DIARY
INTELLIGENCE SUMMARY

Army Form C. 2118.

Ref. Map.
France. Sheet 57c. Scale 1:40,000

Place	Date	Hour	Summary of Events and Information	Remarks and references to Appendices
LITTLE WOOD, YPRES	1-6-17 to 8-6-17		The Field Coy front extending from TRESCAULT inclusive to the CANAL exclusive was maintained by 2 Field Coy's in the line, the 427th Coy being on the left, the 429th Coy on the right with 429th Coy in reserve. The policy of this Division, as shown in Gnl Order No 22 (Appendix A attached) was one of "peaceful penetration" and to this end the two field Coys assisted the Infantry Bdes in the line in the siting of trenches and wire, and supervised the construction of same. On the right the enemy offered resistance and the line was advanced only an average of 300 yards.	App. A
			On the evening of the sixth the line on the left was advanced on a front of 1500 yards and a depth of 300 yards. Careful preparations were made by the 427th Coy (see Appendix B attached) with most successful results although a mist hampered the working party of trenches, which had to be done with the aid of a prismatic compass.	App. B
	14-6-17		A length of trench tramway about 1300 yards, 60 cm gauge with 9lb rails, (as shown on Appendix C attached) was commenced by 429th Coy. This necessitated the formation of embankments cuttings and bridges over communication trenches. The maximum gradient of 2% was laid down. Drains were constructed and first loading laid between the rails to enable men to push the trucks without damage to the track.	App. C
	9-6-17 to 14-6-17		Forward Companies engaged in improvement and maintenance of forward trenches; the 256th Tunnelling Coy R.E. in construction of deep dug-outs and sinking of wells in forward areas and the reserve company on water supply and improvement of billets.	
	15-6-17		The 428 Coy came into relieve the 429 Coy relieving it in the right sector the trench tramway was taken over by 427 Coy, who completed it in 30 the twist.	

WAR DIARY

INTELLIGENCE SUMMARY.

(Erase heading not required.)

Ref/Map. France.
Sheet 57c Scale 1:40,000

Army Form C. 2118.

Place	Date	Hour	Summary of Events and Information	Remarks and references to Appendices
YPRES	16-6-17 to 20-6-17		The forward Companies continued trench maintenance work such as drainage of trenches, revetting, machine gun emplacements, together with water supply from the Canal on left and TRESCAULT on right. Any deep dugouts finished were furnished and occupied as soon as they were ready. The reserve Fd. Coy was engaged upon Corps Summer and winter Camps scheme in the divisional area. In addition hot-water spray baths erected at BERTINCOURT, RUYAULCOURT and YPRES; Japanese, old spray and plunge baths erected or in course of erection at BERTINCOURT, Bus, in HAVRINCOURT WOOD and near Canal (J36a) The main Divn R.E Dump at RUYAULCOURT was considerably enlarged and forward dumps commenced at H31 C09 & Q7d75 in left sector and Q4b21 in right sector, all being supplied by Deauville railway, either from MAIN Dump or III Corps dump at YPRES. Extensions of the Deauville System were constructed to points in the forward area.	MM MM MM
3-6-17.			**Casualties** Lt-Col. D.S. MacINNES, CMG. DSO. RE took over duties of ACRE, Major J.G. RIDDICK returned to 6428 Fd Co RE 2/Lieut J.H. SAINT, 426 Fd Co RE Killed in action.	MM
13-6-17 16-6-17 23-6-17			**Reinforcements** 2/Lieut P. MOREEY held to 429 Fd Co, RE 2/Lieut J.F.W WELCH " " 428 " " " 2/Lieut J.H. DART " " 429 " " "	A. Return of Army Troops in forward area B. Trench tramway C. CRE man-nel D. " " " E. CRE orders no 2 MacInnes Lieut-Col for CRE Adj for CRE

APPENDIX A. to
WAR DIARY, HQRE. 1/2D

PA 2A

Copy sent to each Coy.

SECRET

Copy No. 8

42nd DIVISION ORDER No. 22.

26-5-1917.

1. The energies of the Division are to be concentrated simultaneously on the following four objects.

2. (I). HOLD AND STRENGTHEN the present defensive system. The present front line will be the main line of resistance. A defence scheme to come into operation from 6 a.m. June 1st is under preparation, and will be issued shortly in sections. Sections dealing with the action to be taken in case of attack, and a programme of work, will be issued first.

3. (II). PUSH FORWARD and establish ourselves within assaulting distance of the HINDENBURG LINE. Every opportunity is to be taken to push forward and establish a front line approximately 500 yards from the HINDENBURG LINE.

   This advance will be carried out as far as possible by "peaceful penetration", in three or more stages on a definite programme lasting over a period of three or four weeks, details of which will be issued shortly.

   Each stage will be carried out generally on the following system:- A certain number of important tactical localities about 200 yards in advance of the present front line will be selected and thoroughly patrolled for several nights. Saps to connect these up to the front line will be marked out beforehand, and when everything is ready the locality in question will be occupied by strong patrols, wired in, and the connecting sap dug out without delay. These points will then be joined up laterally, by a continuous trench, thus forming a new front line, and the next stage commenced.

   In carrying out the above policy, it is specially important to sieze without delay any points which deny observation to the enemy.

4. (III). HARASS the enemy and cause him loss. Every effort will be made to prevent the enemy establishing any advanced line in front of the HINDENBURG LINE or adopting the same policy as ourselves: he will also be prevented from improving the defences of the HINDENBURG LINE.

   The following means will be used :-
   (a). Artillery, infantry, and machine gun fire by day and night. Each Bde. will organise a scheme of indirect machine gun fire at night on hostile approaches, rendezvous, or centres of activity.
   (b). By active patrolling and the employment of special offensive patrols.
   (c). By minor enterprises, which whenever possible, should be worked into the scheme of advance described in para. 3.

P.T.O.

- 2 -

5. (IV). ORGANISE the Divisional area as an offensive front for an attack on the HINDENBURG LINE. Details for this will be issued shortly. The work to be done under the defence scheme for the establishment of Hd.Qrs., dumps, trench tramways and forward communications, will be arranged, so far as possible, to fit in with this offence scheme.

6. ACKNOWLEDGE on attached slip.

                                                      Major,
                                                   General Staff,
                                                   42nd Division.

DISTRIBUTION as follows :-

Copy No. 1. File.	Copy No. 8. Divnl. Engineers.
2. War Diary.	9. A.A. & Q.M.G.
3. War Diary.	10. XV Corps.
4. 125th Brigade.	11. XV Corps.
5. 126th Brigade.	12. III Corps.
6. 127th Brigade.	13. 59th Divn.
7. Divnl. Arty.	14. 48th Divn.

Issued by D.R. at 11.30 a.m. 26/5/17.
          Orderly

Appendix B to
War Diary, HQRE.
42 Dvn. for June 1917

H.Q.,
42ND (E.L.) DIVISION,
R.E.
No. CRE 31/6
Date..................

Copies to
427 & 49
for information

Chief Engineer,
III Corps.

The attached copy of report upon the laying out of a new fire trench in the left brigade sector is forwarded as it reflects credit upon Major Mousley for the successful organisation of the work, and upon the subalterns* who laid out the tape by means of compass alone, the night being too misty to pick up any of the landmarks previously selected.

* Lts. Watkinson & Bogle

Lieut. Col. R.E.,
a/C.R.E., 42nd Division.

26/6/17.

COPY.

To C.R.E., 42nd Division.
From O.C., 427 Field Co. R.E.

Subject:- The advance made by 127th Bde. on
night 8/9th June, 1917.

1. **Objective.** Was to establish a new line length about 1,500 yards across the whole Brigade Front at an average distance of 300 yards in front of the existing firing line. The Line to be dug deep enough to man with Lewis Guns and 1 section of rifle men for their protection at 12 points G. to S., the remainder to be spitlocked so as to show a continuous parapet by day to the enemy. A single wire fence of concertina barbed wire (and if possible a second) to be erected along the whole front. The whole of the above to be done in one night.

2. **Preparations.**

(a) **Reconnaissance.** On night of 6/7th June, the ground on the left sector was reconnoitred by 1 section officer and the position on top of the spoil heap on the left flank was taped out as the ground was chalk and there was no possibility of the tape shewing by day. The general line of the trench, to the S. of the spoil heap, was fixed upon and definite objects picked out and rough bearings taken on these objects. The centre of the line was fixed and on the night of 7/8th June a reconnaissance was made of the right sector by the section officer concerned and the point of junction between the left and right sectors fixed.

(b) Each Battalion established a factory to make the necessary number of barbed concertina coils (after demonstration by R.E.), and at some point in their front each Battalion formed a dump of necessary material for the wiring of their section. Excess manufactured was to strengthen the existing front and support lines each night under R.E. supervision so as to perfect the infantry in the drill.

(c) Two days before, the attached table was prepared and any necessary material or tools supplied to Battalions during the night previous to the advance.

3. Organisation

The front was divided into four Battalion sectors, each battalion to complete its own digging and wiring. One F.E. Officer with his section was detailed to each half of this line, and made responsible for the direction of the line.

4. Performance.

With the exception of the length/on the left flank, which *on the spoil heap* was marked out on the night 6/7th, the whole line was marked out before the infantry arrived. The two F.E. Officers and 10 N.C.Os. and sappers proceeded with the covering parties at 10 p.m. and went out to the centre of the new line and then worked to the right and left respectively. A thick mist obscured the ground so the continuous line of tape was laid with the aid of a prismatic compass. The right side of each traverse was marked by a flash about 18" in length attached to the tape. The battalions were held responsible for the length and width of the traverses and to ensure this one battalion set out short lengths of tape equal to the length of a traverse at the correct width (10') from the main tracing tape at each flash point. The N.C.Os. and sappers assisted the infantry in wiring and keeping the right direction of same.

Time Marking out commenced at   10 p.m.
           ,,   ,,   finished at   11-15 p.m.
           Digging & Wiring commenced at 11-30 and 11-15 p.m.
           Working parties withdrawn between 2-15 a.m. and 3-15 a.m.

Results. A continuous line of parapet (except for one gap of about 50 yds.) shown to the enemy, and 12 posts for Lewis Guns and one section of riflemen dug deep enough for occupation throughout the day. On succeeding nights the C.Ts. to this line were dug and the line itself widened and deepened, also the wire strengthened with a second row of concertina wire placed 10 yards behind the first.

Notes.

(a) Trace of Trench :-

(b) To peg down the tape 6" and 6" nails were used.

(c) It was found that one coil of barbed wire made up into concertina wire gave an average length of 8 yards when pulled out, the diameter being about 3 ft.

(d) The carrying parties for the wire had to carry an average of about 450 yards, the size of these parties being $1\frac{1}{2}$ times the wiring party. If this had been increased to two carrying to one wiring two rows of concertina wire could have been put up.

(e) It was found that longer flashes at the traverse points would have been better as the grass was long and the night misty.

                                              (Sgd.) J. H. MOUSLEY,
                                                    Major, R.E.

24/6/17.

TABLE OF TOOLS & STORES.

Note:—

Wiring Tools assume 1 man wiring to 1½ men carrying. Wiring Materials assume double concertina wire fence with diagonal and loose wire between fences as in 4th Army drill assuming barbed concertina coils only expand to 8 yards.

Following stores assumed as required per 8 yard coil of barbed concertina wire:—
1 coil barbed concertina wire.
2 high screw pickets.
1 low screw picket.
2 French Wire staples.
1/6th coil barbed wire.
Entrenching tool helves make excellent windlass sticks.

Digging tools assume each man to carry a shovel or a pick except with 5th Manchesters on chalk pit, when 15 extra picks are allowed.

(Sgd.) J.H.HOUSLEY,
Major,
O.C., 427 Fld. Co.,R.E.
6/6/17.

Battalion.	Frontage in yards.	Total men	Covering Party	Wiring & Carrying	Digging	Tapes, Tracing	Shovels	Picks	Gloves prs.	Wirecutters, prs.	Windlassing sticks	Barbed wire, coils.	Barbed Concertina wire, coils.	French wire, staples.	High Screw Pickets.	Low Screw Pickets.	Plain wire.
5th.	300	200	-	80	120	10	75	90	17	7	17	40	80	160	160	80	-
6th.	250	200	-	50	150	10	75	75	17	7	17	40	80	160	160	80	-
7th.	450	400	-	100	300	20	300	100	35	15	35	60	120	240	240	120	-
8th.	450	400	-	100	300	20	150	150	35	15	35	60	120	240	240	120	-
Totals.	1450	1200	-	330	870	60	600	415	104	44	104	200	400	800	800	400	-

For single Concertina Wire Fence units require materials as below:—

5th										7	40	80	80	40	60
6th										7	40	80	80	40	60
7th										10	60	120	120	60	
8th										10	60	120	120	60	
TOTALS										34	200	400	400	200	

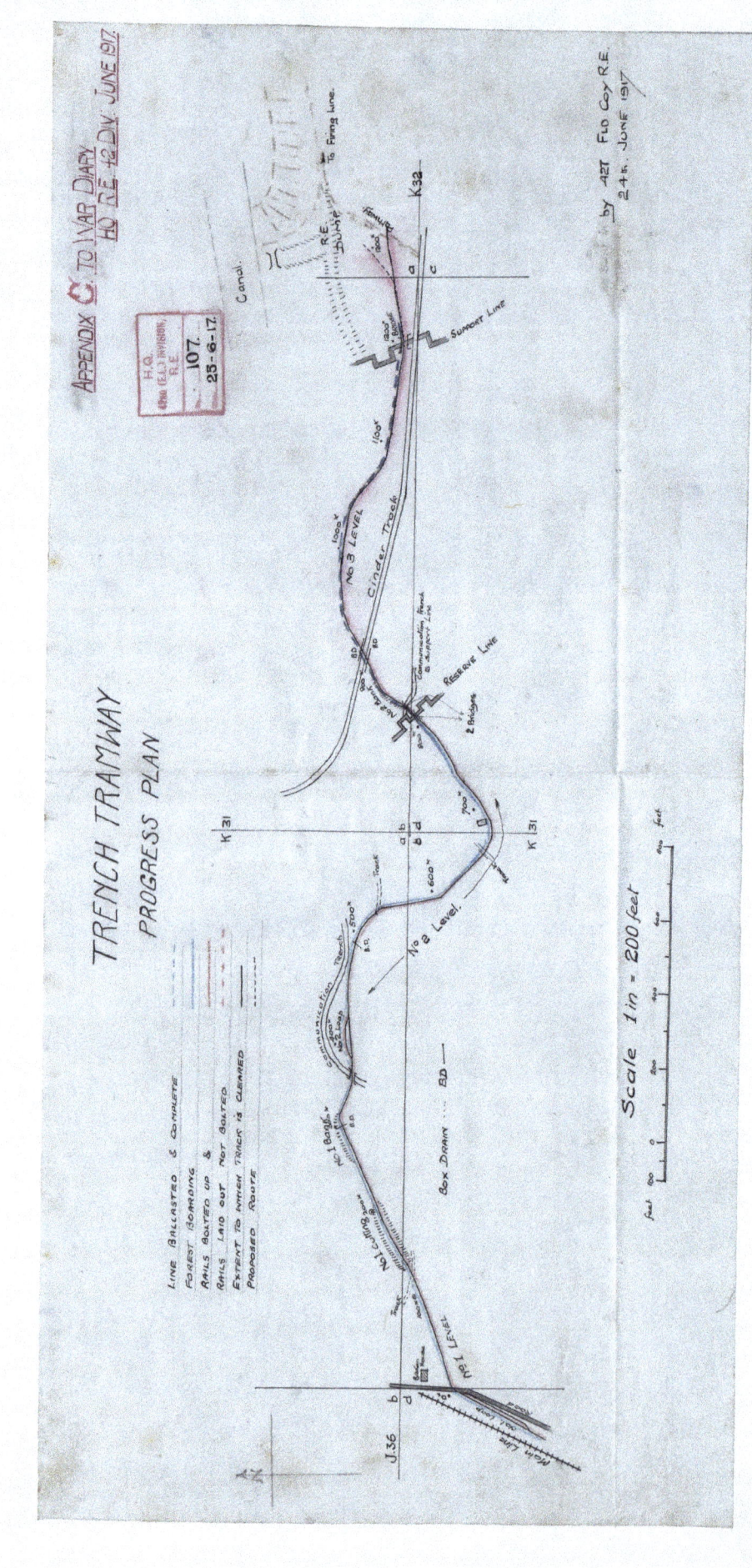

COPY No. 5.

C.R.E., 42nd (E. Lancs.) DIVISION, ORDER No. 1.

- by -

Lt. Col. D.S. MACINNES, C.M.G., D.S.O., R.E.

19th June, 1917.

EXPLOSIVES.

1.   On no account will derelict or 'dud' explosives, shells, bombs, grenades, etc. be handled by any W.O., N.C.O. or man except

    (a) In the course of duty.

    (b) When it is necessary for public safety, e.g., in the case of a bomb lying in a roadway, when it would be put into a place of safety.

2.   No attempt must be made to remove the fuse or detonator from any shell, bomb, etc. except under definite orders by a superior officer.

3.   Men should be warned that if they are injured by the explosion of a shell or bomb, incurred through the disobedience of the above orders, they will be tried by a Field General Court Martial.

A. Norman Walker
Lieut. R.E.,
Adjt. for C.R.E., 42nd Divn.

DISTRIBUTION :-   Copy No. 1 to 427 Field Co. R.E.
                       ,,   2   428 Field Co. R.E.
                       ,,   3   429 Field Co. R.E.
                       ,,   4   File.
                       ,,   5   War Diary.

Copy No. 4

C.R.E., 42nd (E. Lancs.) DIVISION ORDER No. 2.

- by -

Lt.-Col. D. S. MACINNES, C.M.G., D.S.O., R.E.

27th June, 1917.

AWARD.

The C.R.E. has much pleasure in announcing that the Distinguished Conduct Medal has been awarded to No. 440251, Corporal L. CLIFFE, 428th (E. Lancs.) Field Co. R.E.

Lieut. R.E.
Adjt. for C.R.E. 42nd Divn.

Distribution Normal.

Confidential. Original.

Vol 6

War Diary
of
H.Q. R.E. 42nd (E.L.) Div"
from 1st to 31st July. 1917.

(Volume 4.)

WAR DIARY
or
INTELLIGENCE SUMMARY

(Erase heading not required.)

Army Form C. 2118

Refilloh. France. Sheet 57c & 57d
Scale 1: 40,000

Place	Date	Hour	Summary of Events and Information	Remarks and references to Appendices
YTRES	1-7-17 to 4-7-17		H.Q.R.E. employed mainly on preparations for handing over work to C.R.E. 58th Division.	nil
	4-7-17		428 Bdlr. R.E. concentrated at YTRES and was inspected by Brig. Gen. Schreiber, C.B., A.D.C., C.R.E. III Corps.	nil
	5-7-17		428 Co. R.E. marched to New Area, ½ Company to BIHUCOURT, ½ Company to GOMIECOURT.	nil
	6-7-17			nil
	7-7-17		429 and 427 Cos R.E. was inspected by Brig. Gen. Schreiber in MAVRINCOURT WOOD. 429 Co. concentrated at YTRES	nil
	8-7-17		429 Co. R.E. march to New Area, 427 Co. R.E. 4 miles out of the line.	nil
	9-7-17		H.Q.R.E. moved to ACHIET LE PETIT, 429 Co. R.E. arrived ACHIET LE PETIT.	nil
ACHIET LE PETIT.	10-7-17		427 Co. R.E. arrives GOMIECOURT. 2 Sections of 428 Co. R.E. march from GOMIECOURT to BIHUCOURT.	nil
	11-7-17		428 Co. R.E. moved to COURCELLES.	nil
	12-7-17 to 31-7-17		H.Q.R.E. employed in organising and superintending the training (especially in offensive warfare) of the field companies. 429 and 427 Cos R.E. in turn were sent to camp near BERCOURT SUR ANCRE for 2 days for the purpose of training in bridging, both pontoon and improvised over the River ANCRE and its inundations. 428 Co. R.E. erected a bridge over Nandy pond near MIRAUMONT. Minor Engineer services were also carried out during this period e.g. improvements in billets, baths etc.	See App A See App B7c See App D nil
			Casualties.	Miraumont
	5-7-17		Cap' W. Bland, 1.429 Co. R.E. appointed Bde Major 176th Bde	27.7.17 Cap' S.E. Rigg, R.A.M.C. appointed M.O. 428 & 429 ORE (14.7.17) reported to duty H.R.E.
			Reinforcements	
	26-7-17		Lieut. P.Y. Hughes R.E. reported to duty from Base, posted 429 Co. R.E.	A.N.Duncan Lt. Col. C.R.E. Add for C.R.E.

COPY.   Appendix A (sheet 1)

C.R.E.13/7.

O.C.,
427, 428, 429 Field Co. R.E.

TRAINING.

DISMOUNTED MEN.

1. All R.E. Services required in Brigade Camps are to be pushed on with as quickly as possible, and should be completed by Friday evening, 13th instant at latest.

2. Training will commence on the completion of R.E. services, allowing an interval of one day for washing and cleaning up purposes and a kit inspection.

3. The following gives an outline of the system of training to be adopted. It has been drawn up in accordance with Appendix 13, Instructional Training for British Armies in France.

    (a) 7-30 a.m.)   For 8 days.
        to   )   Company parade as strong as possible.
      8-0 a.m.)   Company Drill and Ceremonial.
                   A definite progressive programme from Squad Drill without Arms up to Company Movements will be arranged.

    (b) 9-30 a.m.)   For first 5 days only.
        to   )   1. Musketry.
      1-0 p.m.)   2. Physical training and bayonet fighting.
                   3. Gas Drill.

    (c) 2-30 p.m.)   For 8 days.
        to   )   1. Pontoon Drill as far as is possible without water.
      4-0 p.m.)
                   2. Laying out of strong points. Section Commanders to be responsible for getting out all details of tools, stores and working parties that would be required.
                   3. Laying out a trench at night by aid of prismatic compass.
                   4. Making of "Bangalore" torpedoes or other forms of explosive charge for blowing gaps in wire entanglements.
                   5. Rapid Wiring.

    (d) 4 p.m.   For 8 days.
                  Recreation organised by Officers.

    (e) 6-30 p.m.)   For 8 days.
        to   )   Refreshing Officers and N.C.O.s for the next day's work.
      7-30 p.m.)
                   Conferences amongst Officers and N.C.O.s or lectures by Officers Commanding Companies or Sections on :—
                   1.
                   2. Organisation and leading of carrying parties.
                   3. Consolidation of captured ground, including construction of strong points and defence of craters.
                   4. Blowing up of hostile dug-outs, emplacements &c.
                   5. Temporary bridging expedients.

    (f) 9-30 a.m.)   For last 4 days;
        to   )   Available for subjects mentioned previously in sub-para. (c).
      1-0 p.m.)

4. Company Commanders will send in to this Office by 9-0 a.m. on THURSDAY, 12th instant, programme showing :-

    (a) Detailed scheme and Time Table for (a) and (b).

    (b) Schedule of Training proposed for (c) and (f), taking into consideration their experience of the efficiency of their Companies in each of these subjects, and consequently devoting more time to some items than to others.

5. WEDNESDAYS and SATURDAYS will be considered as half holidays.

MOUNTED MEN.

6. There should be two Mounted Parades between now and SUNDAY 22nd instant, when special attention is to be paid to obtaining a clean turn-out of Horses, Harness, and Men. The C.R.E. will be notified of these Parades.

7. The Drivers must be smartened up and given Squad Dismounted Drill daily either by Sections or as a whole as considered most suitable ny Company Commanders. Particular attention is to be given to Stable Duties.

8. A Lecture should be given to the Drivers as a whole on the principal points in Horse Management.

                                            (Sgd.) D. S. MACINNES,
                                                Lt. Colonel, R.E.
                                            a/C.R.E., 42nd Division.

10/7/1917.

Copy to 42nd Division for information.

COPY.   Appendix A. (sheet 3).

O.C. 427
    429 Field Co. R.E.
----428------------------

      On completion of bridging, work should be carried out on the following lines.

(1). Any men due for inoculation to be inoculated.

(2). Either the morning (9-30 a.m. to 1-0 p.m.) or the afternoon (2-30 p.m. to 4 p.m.) to be devoted to infantry exercises, drill, bayonet fighting, musketry, and the remainder of the working hours to military engineering, subject to modifications to meet requirements of 125, 126, 127 Infantry Brigades or to schemes being set by you, or from H.Q. Divl. R.E. for day or night exercises.

      The training in military engineering is to be devoted to work required in the offensive :-

  (a). Location and laying out of strong points and erection of barbed wire round them.

  (b). Blocking of communication trenches and their defence against bombing attacks.

  (c). Preparation of loads and organisation of carrying parties.

  (d). Destruction of wire entanglements.

  (e). Destruction of dug-outs.

  (f). Organisation of machine gun positions - emplacements and dug-outs.

      Please submit programme for another 8 days.

      I propose to reserve Tuesday 31st instant for a scheme set by me.

                          (Sgd.) D.S. MACINNES,
                                Lieut. Col. R.E.,
                        C.R.E., 42nd Division.

Sent to 429 Co. on 24/7/1917.

To 427 and 428 Cos. on 26th/7/1917.

Appendix A. Sheet 3.

SCHEME FOR LAYING-OUT STRONG POINTS
- for -
428 Field Co. R.E.

CRE 13/54

1. Situation.

The Division is holding a portion of the line facing South West running through GOMMEVILLE, the Divisional front extending from A.7.central to the South-West corner of GOMMEVILLE, A.18.c.9.0. The German front line faces it at 100 to 200 yards' distance.

Orders have been issued for the Division to attack, Zero hour being fixed for noon on 1st August, and final objective being German Reserve Line immediately East of REGAINCOURT.

2. O.C. 428 Field Co. R.E. receives the following instructions :-

(a). Position of Assembly. With reference to Divisional Operation Order No......, the 428 Field Co. R.E. with attached infantry will assemble at A.18.d.1.2. at 11.30 a.m. on the 1st proximo.

(b). Work required. The Company will be organised for the following work :-

Two sections to construct a strong point for a garrison of 1 platoon and 1 machine gun, in support of the left flank of the line to be consolidated by the Infantry, approximate location A.10.a.3.1. (Garrison to be found under arrangements made by O.C., - Brigade).

The attached Infantry to be employed with these sections as carrying party for stores for wire entanglement.

Headquarters and 2 sections to remain in reserve, but to be organised with a view to assisting the Infantry in consolidating the main line if required and more particularly repairs and opening up of enemy dug-outs as Company posts, etc.

(c). Tools and stores to be provided. Tools and stores to be carried by the Royal Engineers and attached Infantry to be at the discretion of O.C., Company, who will make all arrangements for drawing of stores. The attached Infantry will not do more than two journeys.

(d). Transport. Arrangements may be made for employment of pack transport as far as the present firing line, but beyond it stores will be carried by men.

(e). O.C., 428 Field Company will report the arrival of his company at position of assembly personally to Brigade Commander, - Brigade, at -   , and come under the latter's orders as to further action.

Reports to Headquarters, - Brigade as may be ordered by it.

3. With reference to the above note 2 :-

(a). As no attached Infantry are available the remaining two sections of 428 Field Co. will be employed as carrying party.

(b). Barbed wire entanglement will not be erected, but a single line of barbed wire will be put up to represent the line selected.

- 2 -

3. (Cont.).

(c). The trenches for the strong point will be dug to such a depth and width as is possible in a single night.

(d). The exercises will commence at 6-0 p.m. on 1st proximo, C.R.E. representing the Brigade Commander with Headquarters at 418 Field Company's Camp.

(Sgd.) D.S. McIver,

Lieut. Colonel, R.E.,

C.R.E., 42nd Division.

6-0 p.m.,
31st July, 1917.

C.R.E.13/33. Appendix B
sheet 1.

O.C.,
   429 Field Co. R.E.

    Herewith 4 copies of scheme of bridging which you should work to for the first day's bridging operations on the right bank of the ANCRE.

    Local material will not include any material within the Railway yard or any material that forms part of a standing portion of a permanent building such as the mill. Only loose material to be taken.

    You may assume that any approach roads to the bridges are carried out by a separate Infantry party.

                               (Sgd.) D.S.MACINNES,
                                    Lt. Col., R.E.,
                               C.R.E., 42nd Division.

20/7/1917.

Appendix B.
Sheet 2.

H.Q.
42ND (E.L.) DIVISION.
R.E.
No. CRE 13/33
Date.

Scheme for Training in Bridging for 429 Field Company R.E.

On the night of the 20th/21st July the Division reaches the right bank of the ANCRE, about BEAUMONT-HAMEL.

Scouts pushed out to the left bank of the river have gained the heights on that side of the river and have reported all clear.

O.C., 429 Field Co. R.E. receives the following instructions from C.R.E.:-

Bridges across the River ANCRE on the BEAUMONT-HAMEL - ST.PIERRE-DIVION Road have been destroyed and there is a gap of approximately 75 yards in the causeway across the flooded area immediately East of the bridge across the river. This gap has been made impassable by iron girders and other obstructions thrown in and which would have to be cleared before the ~~bridge~~ repairs could be undertaken. Bridges must therefore be to one side of the road.

(A) You will provide bridges for infantry in file across the river and across the flooded area clear of the roadway. The bridges to be ready for use by 8 p.m. on 22nd. 23.00 / 6 a.m.

(B) At the same time you will take steps to commence bridges for Artillery and transport in so far as this can be done without interfering with the completion of the infantry Bridges.

You will have at your disposal your own and the 427 Field Company's bridging equipment and you can make use of any local material including that to be found in the dump on the West side of the main ALBERT - ACHIET-LE-GRAND Road.

The pontoons should be used in the first place for the Infantry Bridge, but in designing for the Artillery Bridge you can assume that you will be able to dismantle the Infantry Bridge so as to make the pontoons and trestles (if you have used these latter) available for the artillery bridges.

In order not to interfere with the passage of infantry you should endeavour to complete a ~~foot~~ temporary bridge over the river for your own purposes in connection with the preparations for the artillery bridge over the flooded area.

Report to me fully by 8-0 a.m. on 22nd the action you are taking.

(Signed)

C.R.E.13/38.

Appendix C
Sheet 1.

O.C.,
427 Field Co. R.E.

The attached is the scheme upon which you should work during your two days' bridging on the River ANCRE.

The gap of 75 yards in the causeway will be taken to extend from the Western edge of the flooded area Eastwards, there being water on both sides of the road and all trees gone.

Materials must not be taken from the Railway Yard or standing buildings demolished for the purpose,- only loose materials to be used.

(Sgd.) D.S. MACINNES,
Lt. Col., R.E.,
C.R.E., 42nd Division.

23/7/1917.

Appendix C.
Sheet 2.

Scheme for Training in Bridging for 427 Field Co. R.E.

On the morning of the 24th July the Division moving from West to East reaches the right bank of the River ANCRE about BEAUMONT-HAMEL.

Scouts pushed out to the left bank of the River have gained the heights on that side and reported all clear.

O.C., 427 Field Co. R.E. receives the following instructions from C.R.E.:-

The Bridges across the River ANCRE on the BEAUMONT-HAMEL-ST.PIERRE-DIVION Road have been destroyed and there is a gap of approximately 75 yards in the causeway across the flooded area immediately East of the bridge across the River. This gap has been made impassable by iron girders and other obstructions thrown in. These obstructions would have to be cleared before a bridge could be built on the line of the road. Bridges must therefore be to one side.

It is the intention to secure the ground occupied by us on the left bank of the river with the least possible delay. Infantry and Artillery to cross as early as possible.

You will act as follows :-

(a)   Provide means for getting Infantry across the flooded area as quickly as possible by raft, using pontoon rafts until they are required for the bridge, and any improvised rafts you think would be of value. Arrangements for the Infantry to cross to be completed not later than 6 p.m. on the 25th instant. A bridge for infantry in file has already been constructed over the ANCRE.

(b)   You will construct bridges for infantry and Field Artillery across the River ANCRE and the flooded area.

The shore ends of the bridge should be designed with a view to their use if necessary - after strengthening - as landing stages for rafting 60 pounder guns across by pontoon rafts, the pontoon portion of the bridge being used for the rafts.

The bridge to be completed by 12 noon on the 26th instant.

You will have for this purpose the pontoon equipment of the three field companies, and you can make use of any local material including that to be found in the dump on the West side of the main ALBERT - ACHIET LE GRAND Road.

Report to me fully by 8 a.m. 25th instant what arrangements you are making and what sized unit/you would like to have ready close to the Landing Stage for rafting over at any one time.

An assembly place for infantry is being formed immediately West of the Railway Station.

(Sgd.) D.S.MACINNES,
Lt. Col. R.E.,
C.R.E., 42nd Division.

6-30 p.m.
23 July, 1917.

Appendix D.
Sheet 1.

O.C.,
    428 Field Co. R.E.

    Please arrange to carry out the enclosed scheme which is intended as an exercise for your officers in :-
    (1) Reconnaissance with the object of using local material.
    (2) Planning of the work so that not more material is collected than is required for the construction of the bridge with a small margin.
    (3) The careful organisation of working parties in the actual construction.

    Where the work requires nothing more than a plank roadway you can assume that the work will be carried out by an Infantry working party, and you need not make provision for the material.

    If there is difficulty in collecting sufficient material for the planking of the roadway this can be represented by planks at intervals instead of continuous work.

                                  (SGD.) D.S.MACINNES,
                                        Lieut. Col., R.E.,
                                    C.R.E., 42nd Division.

23/7/1917.

Appendix D.
Sheet 2.

Scheme for Training in Causeway and Bridging Work for 428 Field Co. R.E.

The Division is holding a portion of a line running through ACHIET LE GRAND - BUCQUOY and facing a German Line running through COURCELLES - ABLAINZEVELLE.

C.R.E. issues the following instructions to O.C., 428 Field Company R.E:-

A Battery of 60 pounder B.L.B. Guns is to be established in the valley about L.23.d.9.9. (57.d. 1/40,000). It will be brought up along the main road through MIRAUMONT, and in order to get it into position it will be necessary for it to cross the ditch in the marshy ground immediately West of the Road in 24.a., 50 to 100 yards North of the Bridge on the main road.

You will be responsibl- reconnoitre and arrange for a causeway to be built across the ditch referred to, using such loose materials as you can obtain from the village of MIRAUMONT, or from the old German Pioneer Dump about ¼ mile South of the bridge referred to above.

You will employ a construction similar to that used for the bridge on the main road.

The causeway should be completed by midnight 26th/27th July.

(SGD.) D.S. MACINNES,
Lt. Colonel,
C.R.E., 42nd Division.

23/7/1917.

Vol E 7

WAR DIARY
of
H.Q. R.E., 42nd (E. Lancs) Div.n T.F.
from 1st to 31st August. 1917.

(Volume 4).

Confidential.
ORIGINAL

WAR DIARY
INTELLIGENCE SUMMARY

(Erase heading not required.)

Army Form C. 2118

Reference Maps.
France Sheets. 57 C and d. 1:40,000
Belgium " 27 and 28. 1:40,000

Place	Date	Hour	Summary of Events and Information	Remarks and references to Appendices
ACHIET LE PETIT	1-8-17 to 20-8-17		H.Q.R.E. occupied in organisation of training of the Field Coys R.E., consisting chiefly in laying out of strong points both isolated and in conjunction with Brigade schemes. Experiments were made with bangalore torpedoes and in the best methods of carrying R.E. stores in active operations both on pack animals and on men.	JMN
ACHEUX. AVELUY.	21-8-17.		H.Q.R.E. proceeded to ACHEUX by road and was billeted there.	JMN
	22-8-17.		Left ACHEUX and proceeded by road to AVELUY, rested during the day with 429 Field Coy. R.E. between AVELUY and BOUZINCOURT.	JMN
	23-8-17.		H.Q.R.E. left camp at 1.30 a.m., entrained at AVELUY station, detrained at 1 p.m. at HOPOUTRE near POPERINGHE (Belgium), marched by road to WATOU and was billeted there.	JMN
WATOU	24-8-17 to 30.8.17		H.Q.R.E. arranged for the taking over the front held by 15th Division.	JMN
	31.8.17.		H.Q.R.E. marched by road to BRANDHOEK (Sheet 28. J.7074) and took over from C.R.E. 15th Division at 10 a.m.	JMN

Waller
A. Newman Capt RE. & Bnt
Capt RE. H.Q. 42 Div
Adjt for CRE.

Vol 8

WAR DIARY.
OF
H.Q.R.E. 42(E.L.) Div.
from 1st to 30th Sept. 1917.

(Volume 4)

Confidential
AR 161 NAL

WAR DIARY

INTELLIGENCE SUMMARY

Army Form C. 2118.

Instructions regarding War Diaries and Intelligence Summaries are contained in F. S. Regs., Part II. and the Staff Manual respectively. Title pages will be prepared in manuscript.

(Erase heading not required.)

Reference maps: Belgium. Sheet 28. 1/40,000
Sheet 27. 1/40,000

Place	Date	Hour	Summary of Events and Information	Remarks and references to Appendices
BRAN	1-9-17 to 3-9-17		Three Field Companies in YPRES. Companies being accommodated in YPRES and the remaining Coy at BRANDHOEK. The 267th Field Coy R.E. was attached to us and was billeted in YPRES. Work was done on the duck board tracks, strong points, maintenance of roads, accommodation in YPRES and drainage of deep dug-outs.	
	4-9-17		427 & 428 Fd. Coys R.E. were preparing for the attack to be made by 125 Bde on BORRY, BEEK HOUSE and IBERIAN FARMS. Wiring materials were carried forward by night and arranged in dumps behind the front line ready to be captured forward after the capture of the objectives.	
	5-9-17		Gas shell attack on the RAMPARTS, YPRES. Casualties in 3 Fd. Coys amounted to 28 O.R.	Appendix A
	6-9-17		125 Bde attacked. A report showing the work done by the Field Companies is attached.	
	7-9-17 to 15-9-17		Work carried on as above, prior to attack. Work mainly on duck board tracks, fitting fascines, improving aid posts and Battalion Hdqrs, draining out concrete dug-outs in old German Lines.	
	16-9-17		428 Fd. Coy moved from YPRES to transport lines at BRANDHOEK, and 429 Fd Co did the same.	
	17-9-17		427 " " " " " " " 429 Fd Co moved from BRANDHOEK to BUSSEBOOM (G 15 a 0 1)	
POPERINGHE	18-9-17		HQ R.E. moved to POPERINGHE being relieved by 9th Bn. R.E. Night work on the YPRES-MENIN Road done by the 428 Fd Co R.E. who were sent forward by motor lorry for this purpose. of camouflage screens	
	19-9-17		427 Fd. Co. R.E. moved to ST. JAN TER BEZEN; 428 Fd Co. by motor lorry to WINNEZEELE	
	20-9-17		429 Fd. Co. moved by march route to WINNEZEELE AREA	
	21-9-17		429 Fd. Co. moved to WORMHOUDT with 126 Bde. 429 Fd. Coys transport left on route for COXYDE	

Army Form C. 2118.

WAR DIARY
or
INTELLIGENCE SUMMARY.
(Erase heading not required.)

Reference maps. Belgium. Sheet 11 & 12. 1/40,000

Place	Date	Hour	Summary of Events and Information	Remarks and references to Appendices
LA PANNE	22-9-17		HQ RE moved from POPERINGHE to LA PANNE. 427 2nd Co. R.E. moved by train to ARNEKE, & transport by road; 428 2nd Co. by march route to TETEGHEM area. 429 2nd Co. by motor bus to CANADA CAMP, COXYDE.	MM MM
	23-9-17		428 2nd Co. moved by march route to LA PANNE.	MM
	24-9-17		427 " " " train (transport by road) to GHYVELDE, 428 2nd Co. by march route to OOST DUNKERQUE BAINS relieving 430 2nd Co RE, and 419 2nd Co. to NIEUPORT BAINS taking over from the 432 2nd Co R.E. HQ RE moved to ST IDESBALD, relieving 66th Bri RE. a/s A.	MM
ST IDESBALD	25-9-17		427 2nd Co. moved to OOST DUNKERQUE BAINS, taking over from 431 2nd Co R.E. 429 2nd Co. RE Survey Section forward for work on tramways. Work commenced on repair and upkeep of roads, subways, camouflage screens, construction of emplacements.	MM
	26-9-17		Work as above, also maintenance of trenches, fitting of gas blankets, construction of advanced	MM
	30-9-17		AHQ, base standings in LA PANNE district.	

A. Nohuson Walker
Capt RE
Adjt 42 Div R.E.
for CRE 42 Div

Report on R.E. Work carried out in connection with
Operations against IBERIAN, BECK HOUSE and
BORRY FARM.

***App. A.
WAR DIARY. HQRE
Sept 1917***

IBERIAN.

Six wiring parties each consisting of one sapper and nine Infantry men were organised and trained, and were put under the supervision of 1 R.E. Officer, 1 Infantry Officer and 1 R.E. N.C.O.

The carrying party was composed of 2 Infantry Officers and 60 Infantry men.

The wiring parties assembled in DUST TRENCH (D.19.a.).

The carrying party assembled in trenches about C.30.d.7.9.

The dump of wiring materials was at D.19.c.7.8.

No material was sent forward and no work was done since the Infantry failed to reach their objective.

Casualties. R.E. 1 Officer killed.   1 Other Rank killed.
Infantry.   7 Other ranks

BECK HOUSE.

A wiring party consisting of 1 R.E. Officer, 1 Infantry Officer, 1 R.E. N.C.O., 6 Sappers and 18 Infantry men assembled in the vicinity of LOW FARM.

A carrying party of 1 Infantry Officer and 25 Other ranks assembled in trenches about C.30.d.7.9.

The dump of wiring materials was at LOW FARM, North of the Road.

Orders were received for the wiring party to move forward, but only one sapper reached the farm, the remainder being held up 100 yards West of the Farm.

Casualties.   R.E.   2 sappers killed.   1 sapper wounded.

Note on the Condition of BECK FARM.

It is about the same size as IBERIAN FARM.

The two buildings still exist and also the trench in front of the main building

The roof of the main building is of concrete about 4 feet thick; a passage 8 feet wide runs along the side away from the British Front; the wall facing our front is covered with debris and apparently contains no loopholes or windows.

BORRY FARM.

A party of 1 R.E. Officer and eight other ranks with three officers and 62 other ranks of 126 Brigade Pioneers took part in the above operations in conjunction with 1/5th Battn. Lancs.Fus.

The above parties were all in position by 3 a.m. on the 6th instant, either at LOW FARM or fifty yards S.E. of LOW FARM, where wiring materials for 400 yards High French Wire (IV Army Standard Pattern) had been dumped beforehand and made up in man loads. Three of the sappers were specially detailed - they had had a day's practice beforehand - to work with 3 wiring teams of the 5th Battn. Lancs. Fus.

The Pioneers were all detailed to act as carrying parties from LOW FARM to the objective as soon as it was gained, and the three Officers were made responsible for various portions of that part of the work.

At 5-30 a.m. on the 6th instant, the three wiring squads carried sufficient wiring materials 20 yards forward to complete 90 yards of wire fence.

At Zero, the three wiring squads with the attached sappers went forward the 20 yards from the wiring material dump to the assembly or front line trench, where they were ordered to await orders.

The carrying party at 8-0 a.m. was ordered to move wiring materials forward to an old German Trench 100 yards in front of our front line. Owing to the heavy fire which resulted and consequent casualties, it was found quite impossible to move any materials in front of our front line trench, and owing to casualties even this was not persisted in.

At 9-0 a.m. there was a counter-attack, and those of carrying party who had reached the front line trench stood to, and remained there until 11-30 p.m. 6th instant.

P.T.O.

At 12-15 night of 6th/7th Sept. orders were received to put out 60 yards of wire 150 yards in front of the pres previous front line, to protect a small forward post on the right flank.

The two wiring squads carried their own wire out and completed the work in two hours. During the night, 20 of the Pioneers were detailed to assist in digging this small post.

The R.E? & Pioneers parties received orders to withdraw at 3-0 a.m. on the 7th instant.

Copy No. 8

C.R.E., 49nd (N. MIDLAND) DIVISION ORDER NO. 18.

– by –

LIEUT. COLONEL D. S. MACINNES, C.M.G., D.S.O., R.E.

Reference Map. BELGIUM, Sheet 28.   16th Septr., 1917.

1.   Under instructions from Vth Corps, the 16th Battalion, Royal Irish Rifles (Pioneers) will not be attached to the 9th Division but will concentrate in BRANDHOEK, No. 2 Area at H.7.c.5.3. for a period of rest.

2.   The two companies at present in YPRES will not work after the night 16th/17th and will rejoin their Battalion at H.7.c.5.3. on 17th instant, the movement to be completed by 8-0 p.m.

They will hand over work in progress to O.C. 9th Seaforth Regt. (Pioneers).

3.   The two companies at present in Reserve will not work on jobs in the BRANDHOEK Area after the 17th instant.

Lieut. Colonel, R.E.,
C.R.E., 49nd Division.

DISTRIBUTION:-

Copy Nos. 1 & 2. 16th Batt. R.I.R. (P).
       3.   "G", 49nd Division.
       4.   "Q", 49nd Division.
       5.   C.R.E., 9th Division.
       6.   C.E. Vth Corps.
       7.   Town Major, YPRES.
       8.   War Diary.
       9.   File.

SECRET.

Copy No. 7

C.R.E., 42nd (E. LANCS.) DIVISION, ORDER NO. 17.

- by -

LIEUTENANT COLONEL D. S. MACINNES, C.M.G., D.S.O., R.E.

Reference 1/20,000 Map, Sheets 27N.E., & 28.N.W.   16th Sept., 1917.

---

1. The 42nd Division (less Artillery) is moving from the BRANDHOEK Area to WINNEZEELE, WATOU, and ST. JAN TER BIEZEN Areas on the 19th instant.

2. For the purpose of this move the Field Companies will receive all orders from the G.Os.C. their respective Brigade Groups.

3. H.Q.R.E. will remain at POPERINGHE.

M Walker
Captain, R.E.,
Adjt. for C.R.E., 42nd Division.

DISTRIBUTION :-

Copy No. 1. 427 Fld. Co. R.E.
        2. 428 Fld. Co. R.E.
        3. 429 Fld. Co. R.E.
        4. H.Q., 125 Bde.
        5. H.Q., 126 Bde.
        6. H.Q., 127 Bde.
        7. War Diary.
        8. File.

C. R. E., 42nd (E. Lancs.) Division Order No. 19.

- by -

LIEUT. COLONEL D. S. MACINNIS, C.M.G., D.S.O., R.E.

19th Septr., 1917.

The Divisional Commander has instructed me to express his appreciation of the way in which both Officers, Warrant Officers, N.C.O.s and Men of the Divisional R.E. have carried out their work whilst in the line under trying conditions.

A. N. Walker, Capt. R.E.
for Lieut. Colonel, ...,
C.R.E., 42nd Division.

DISTRIBUTION :- Normal.

Secret

Copy No 4

C.R.E., 42nd (E. Lancs.) Division, Order No. 20a.

- by -

LIEUT. COLONEL D. S. MACINNES, C.M.G., D.S.O., R.E.

20th Septr., 1917.

H.Q.R.E. will close at POPERINGHE at 9-30 a.m. on 22nd inst. and open at WINNEZEELE at the same hour.

A.W.Walker

Captain, R.E.,
Adjt. for C.R.E., 42nd Division.

DISTRIBUTION :- Normal.

ADDENDUM NO. 1 to C.R.E.'s OPERATION ORDER NO. 20.

- by -

LT. COLONEL D. S. MACINNES, C.M.G., D.S.O., R.E.

5th October, 1917.

1.   With reference to para. 4 of C.R.E.'s Operation Order No. 20, the transport of 428 and 429 Field Companies R.E. will remain in their present billets until ~~the~~ mid-day 7th October; the transport of the relieving companies of the 41st Division taking up ~~up~~ the horse lines at OOST DUNKERKE BAINS for the night of 6/7th October.

[signature]

Lieut. Colonel, R.E.,
C.R.E., 42nd Division.

DISTRIBUTION:-
    Copies 1 & 2, File & War Diary.
    Copy 3, O.C. 428 Field Co.
    Copy 4, O.C. 429 Field Co.
    Copy 5, C.R.E., 41st Division.

SECRET.   Copy No..1..

C.R.E., 42nd (E. LANCS.) DIVISION, OPERATION ORDER No. 20.

- by -

LIEUT. COLONEL G. H. MACKENZIE, C.M.G., D.S.O., R.E.

4th October, 1917.

Reference: Coast Administrative Map, 1/100,000.
Special Maps Nos. 4 & 8, 1/10,000.

1. The 42nd Division (less Artillery) will be relieved in the NIEUPORT BAINS Sector and the COXYDE BAINS Coast Defence Sector by the 41st Division (less Artillery) on the 6th Oct. The 42nd Division (less Artillery) will relieve the 32nd Division (less Artillery) in the NIEUPORT SECTOR on the 5th and 6th October.

2. The 125th Infantry Brigade will relieve the 97th Infantry Bde., 32nd Division, in the LOMBARTZYDE Section on the night 5th/6th October, with Headquarters at O.27.b.6.3. The 126th Infantry Bde., after having been relieved in the COXYDE BAINS Coast Defence Sector on the morning of the 6th October by the 124th Infantry Brigade, 41st Division, will relieve the 14th Infantry Brigade, 32nd Division, in the ST. GEORGE'S Section on the night 6th/7th Oct., with Headquarters at Villa Juliette, OOST DUNKERKE. The 127th Infantry Brigade, on relief in the NIEUPORT BAINS Sector by the 123rd Infantry Brigade, 41st Division on the night 6th/7th October, will be in Divisional Reserve, with Headquarters at LA PANNE.

3. Field Coys. R.E., 42nd Division, and Pioneer Battn. 1st Divn., will be relieved by Field Coys. R.E., and Pioneer Battalion, 41st Division, under arrangements to be made by the C.R.E.'s concerned. On relief, the Field Coys. R.E., 42nd Division, and the Pioneer Battn., 1st Division, attached 42nd Division, will relieve the Field Coys. R.E. and the Pioneer Battalion, 32nd Division. Details to be arranged by C.R.E.s concerned. The ultimate arrangements for Field Coys. R.E., 42nd Division, will be :-

    (a). At the disposal of O.O.C., 125th Infantry Brigade - 428th Field Coy. R.E.

    (b). At the disposal of O.O.C., 126th Infantry Brigade -

- 2 -

427th Field Coy. R.E.

(c). At the disposal of C.R.E., 42nd Division, and employed principally on keeping in repair the Bridges at
NIEUPORT — 429th Field Coy. R.E.

4. Field Company and 6th Welsh Regt. (Pioneers) reliefs will be carried out as follows:-

427th Field Coy. R.E. to be relieved by 228th Field Coy. R.E. and to relieve 226th Field Co. R.E. on afternoon of 5th Octr. 1917.

428th Field Coy. R.E. to be relieved by 227th Field Coy. R.E. and to relieve 219 Field Coy. R.E. on afternoon of 6th Octr., 1917.

429th Field Coy. R.E. to be relieved by 233rd Field Co. R.E. and to relieve 218th Field Co. R.E. on afternoon of 6th Octr., 1917.

All above reliefs to be completed by 6-0 p.m. on the dates ordered.

6th Welsh Regt. (Pioneers) to be relieved by 19th Battn. Middlesex Regt. and to relieve the 17th Batt. Northumberland Fusiliers (Pioneers) on the morning of the 7th Octr., relief to be completed by midday.

The location of billets of Field Companies, 42nd Division, and attached Field Coys. R.E. and Pioneers, and of dumps, is given in attached table.

Maison Tricar Dump will be taken over by 428 Field Co. R.E. and REDAN Dump by O.C. 427 Field Co. R.E.

5. All Defence Maps and Plans, Works Drawings etc. applying to Left Divisional Area will be handed over to relieving Companies, and those applying to the Right Divisional Area will be taken over from Companies relieved. Ordinary maps will be retained.

6. Pending further instructions in regard to works programmes, each Field Company and Pioneers will carry on the work of the unit which it relieves. There will be no break in the continuity of work on the bridges, and on the construction of the Dam near Bridge 66.

7. Headquarters, 42nd Divisional R.E. will close at ST. IDESBALD at 10-0 a.m. on 7th October, and re-open at COXYDE BAINS (W.11.b.4.9) at the same hour.

- 3 -

8. ACKNOWLEDGE. (Bde & Pion. Batt. only)

                         D. Maclure
                      Lieut. Colonel, R.E.,
                      C.R.E., 42nd Division.

Copies to :-

1. War Diary.
2. File.
3. 427 Field Co.
4. 428 Field Co.
5. 429 Field Co.
6. 5th Welsh Regt. (Pioneers).
7. 42nd Division 'G'.
8. 42nd Division 'Q'.
9. 125th Inf. Bde.
10. 126th Inf. Bde.
11. ~~127th Inf. Bde.~~
11. C.R.E., 32nd Division.
12. C.R.E., 41st Division.

LOCATION OF FIELD COYS. R.E., 42nd DIVISION,
Attached Pioneer Battalion, and
Attached Field Coys. R.E.

Unit.	Headquarters.	Sections and attached Infantry.	Horse Lines.
Headquarters R.E.	W.11.b.4.9.	-	W.11.b.4.9.
427 Field Co. R.E.	M.34.b.5.5.	M.34.b.55 Inf.M.34.b.5.5.	W.23.central.
429 Field Co. R.E.	M.27.b.4.7.	M.27.b.4.7.	W.16.c.2.2.
428 Field Co. R.E.	X.11.c.3.9.	2 secs. Maison Tricar 2 secs. X.11.c.3.9.	W.23.central.
23rd Field Co. R.E.	X.4.a.2.7.	X.4.a.2.7.	
26th Field Co. R.E.	CANADA CAMP.	CANADA CAMP.	CANADA CAMP.
6th Welsh Regt. (Pioneers).	X.3.b.6.8.	-	-
Wing 2nd A.T. Coy. R.E.	S.9.b.8.3.	S.9.b.8.3.	-

       GLASGOW DUMP   -   X.8.b.6.0.

       HULL DUMP.   -   X.8.b.3.6.

   Forward Dumps.

       Left. KEBAB   -   M.28.c.7.9.

       Right. MAISON TRICAR.   -   M.35.b.2.6.

Map references :-   OOST DUNKIRK   (N & T).   Sheet 11)
                    OSTENDE   (M)   ,, 14) 1/40,000
                    BELGIUM & FRANCE (X)   ,, 19)

Vol 9

WAR DIARY
of
H.Q. R.E. 42nd (E.L.) Division
from 1st to 31st October 1917
(Volume 4).

Confidential
ORIGINAL

WAR DIARY
INTELLIGENCE SUMMARY
(Erase heading not required.)

Army Form C. 2118

Ref. Maps. Belgium. Sheets 11 v 12.
Scale 1:40,000

Place	Date	Hour	Summary of Events and Information	Remarks and references to Appendices
ST. IDESBALD	1-10-17 to 3-10-17		In the left sector of 15th Corps, on the coast, little offensive work carried out in this sector, except the preparation and maintenance of rafts and assault bridging stores to be used in the event of an advance.	MW
	4-10-17		Preparations commenced for handing over to the 41st Division.	MW
	5-10-17		427 Fd. Cy. moved from R.27.c.50 to NIEUPORT	MW
	6-10-17		428 Fd. Cy. moved " Cy. Hdqrs and 2 sections to X.11.c.3.9 and 2 Sections to MAISON TRICAR. 429 " " " to M.27.b.4.7.	MW
	7-10-17		H.Q.R.E. moved from ST. IDESBALD to COXYDE BAINS	MW
COXYDE BAINS	8-10-17 to 17-10-17		The 23rd and 26th Fd. Cos. R.E. and the 6th Batt. the Welsh Regt. Pioneers were attached to 1 Corps Division. The organisation was, one field Cy. to each of the two Infy. Brigades in the line, one field Cy. in charge of the bridges providing communication over the MARITIME YSER, and two Fd. Cys. together with the Battalion of Pioneers for back area work and communications. 2 Sections of the 2nd Army Tramway Cy R.E. were also attached for work on Trench Tramways in the forward area and connecting same with main Neauville System. On the left Sector the principal work was the drainage of the REDAN, where a new escape dam was found necessary and also a tunnelled sluice, and the forward areas on both sides of the LOMBARTZYDE ROAD. On the right Sector the work was mainly that of improving existing tunnels and of constructing machine gun emplacements, OPs etc. the field Cy in this Sector also had charge of the bridges on the right Sector front. On the bridges were constantly being shelled, continuous patrolling was necessary and frequent repair essential. The PUTNEY, CROWDER & VAUXHALL Bridges and the Civil Ports called for the greatest amount of attention.	MW

Army Form C. 2118.

WAR DIARY
INTELLIGENCE SUMMARY.

(Erase heading not required.)

Instructions regarding War Diaries and Intelligence Summaries are contained in F.S. Regs., Part II. and the Staff Manual respectively. Title pages will be prepared in manuscript.

Ref. maps.
Belgium. Sheet 11 —
Scale 1: 40,000

Place	Date	Hour	Summary of Events and Information	Remarks and references to Appendices
COXYDE BAINS.	18-10-17		The 23rd and 26th Madlys RE and the 6th Welsh Pioneers left and the distribution of the RE had to be altered. Back area work came to a standstill.	AW
	19-10-17 to 22-10-17		A section of the night Fd. Cy. was brought back to run the workshops, as the RE troops outside Coxyde out-any urgent jobs in the back area such as the construction of two rooms, one in Coxyde and the other in QUEENSLAND CAMP for the treatment of TRENCH FOOT.	JNW
	23-10-17		The 228th Field Cy. RE was attached together with 1 Coy of the 19th Batt. Middlesex Regt. Reserve.	JNW
	24-10-17 to 27-10-17		A fresh distribution of the field Coys was made. The 226th Fd. Cy. took part in the disposal of the left Brigade thus releasing the 457 Fd. Cy for drainage work and consist of Pamille of the entrance of the EVACUATION CANAL, which was constantly shelled this necessitating frequent and urgent repairs. The section east of the 457 & 228 Fd Coys was detailed for the work of erecting shelter in WELLINGTON CAMP.	JNW
	28-10-17		The 228 Fd. Cy. and the Middlesex Pioneers were suddenly ordered to rejoin their own Division.	HW
	29-10-17		The 83 Det Cy. and 1 Coy of the 9th Battalion Seaforth Highlanders Pioneers were attached and carried on with the work of the units they relieved.	JNW
	30-10-17 to 31-10-17		Usual work carried on.	JNW
			The experience was made to solve the difficulty of satisfying the increasing demands of the Artillery. To this end two Artillery Officers were detailed for liaison work with the RE. one visiting the batteries and ascertaining their requirements and the other dealing with HOPE and receiving the details from the forward Artillery Officer. In conjunction with the Shero Officer RE these three were issued to the battaries who had to do all their own work at the RE recovered was available. Concrete was mixed day at the dump by an infantry working party and sent up nightly to the batteries to be used wet and used for existing Dugout Shelters. The Artillery Officers attached to HOPE controlled stores and handled (personnelly) and the forward RA Officers controlled the distribution. This system is so far working	JNW

A. Norman Watt. Capt No RE

Wt 10

WAR DIARY.

of

H.Q R.E. 42nd (E. Lancs) Division

from 1st to 30th November 1917

(Volume 4)

Confidential
ORIGINAL

Army Form C. 2118.

Reference Maps.
Belgium. Sheets 11 & 12. Scale 1:40,000
" 1:100,000
HAZEBROUCK.

WAR DIARY

INTELLIGENCE SUMMARY.

(Erase heading not required.)

Instructions regarding War Diaries and Intelligence Summaries are contained in F.S. Regs., Part II. and the Staff Manual respectively. Title pages will be prepared in manuscript.

Place	Date	Hour	Summary of Events and Information	Remarks and references to Appendices
COXYDE BAINS	1-11-17 to 15-11-17		H.Q.R.E. employed on organising the work of 4th A. Coys, 1 Coy of 9th Seaforth Highlanders Pioneers. The work consisted of repair work on Dam 66 over Evacuation Canal NIEUPORT and was of a hard and dangerous nature. 407 No.Cs were employed on this, were responsible for some excellent work. The ground to the West and East of the LOMBARTZYDE road was maintained dry and the trenches duckboarded, drained and kept in a good state of repair. The same applies to the trenches in the right sector. Machine Gun concrete emplacements were continued, bridges maintained, roads repaired as far as available labour would allow and screens erected. Towards the end of this period information was received that we should shortly be handing over to the French. Maps, notes etc were begun accordingly.	See Affair. 1
	16-11-17		The Company of Pioneers rejoined its own Division (9th Division). Dam 66 and all RESAN sluices were badly smashed, thus enabling the high tide to undo all the previous work of drainage.	MM
	17-11-17		The 63rd Rd Coy rejoined the 9th Division on the march.	MM
	18-11-17		On night 18th/19th all 3 Road Coys were relieved by French units of 28th Regiment du Genie.	MM
WORMHOUDT	19-11-17		All Coys all on trek to new areas. H.Q.R.E. moved by motor lorry to WORMHOUDT	MM 44.B.
AIRE	20-11-17		H.Q.R.E. moved from WORMHOUDT to AIRE	MM
	22-11-17		H.Q. & 3rd Coy arrived in AIRE Area. Billeted at GLOMENGEN.	MM

WAR DIARY

Reference Map. Army Form C. 2118.
BELGIUM. HAZEBROUCK.
Scale 1:100,000

INTELLIGENCE SUMMARY.
(Erase heading not required.)

Place	Date	Hour	Summary of Events and Information	Remarks and references to Appendices
AIRE.	23-11-17		427 Fd. Co. arrived in AIRE area, billeted at STEENBECQ.	MM
			428 " " " " " " " LA ROGPIE	
	24-11-17 to 25-11-17		Fd Cos all resting paying special attention to the cleaning of men, animals and transport. No training other recreational was attempted.	MM
	26-11-17 to 30-11-17		Fd Cos proceeded by march route to relieve 3rd Cos of 25th Divisional RE in GIVENCHY and GINCHY Sectors. 427 Fd. Co. relieved 106th Fd. Co., and 469 Fd MM Co. relieved #30th Fd. Co. whilst 428 Fd. Co. remained in reserve area and did not relieve 105th Fd. Co. R.E. which continued to work in Glieure right sector not taken over by 42nd Div from 25th Div.	MM. FE.
LOCON			HQ RE moved to LOCON on 29th inst.	

A Norman Walker
Capt & Adjt RE
for CRE
142 Div

REPORT ON DAM 66.   App. A.
                       War Diary. Nov 1917

1. Damage by shell fire.

During the morning of 31/10/17, a breach was made in this Dam about 15 feet wide by 7 feet deep, right in the centre.   About 12-30 p.m. there was a 5 metre high spring tide, which poured through the breach, causing flooding of the EVACUATION CANAL and the area bounded by the NASAL SUPPORT TRENCH, on the East side of the LOMBARTZYDE ROAD.

The Dam, previous to destruction, was made partially of Brick Rubble, with several odd lengths of channel iron, &c. thrown in. On top of the rubble, a reinforced concrete cap had been made, 4 feet deep by about 7 feet wide, which had been commenced about 16/10/17, and had not had sufficient time to thoroughly set, as the cement available for the concrete, requires about 28 days to set hard. This cap was entirely demolished by the shell fire.

2. Organisation for the Repair.

On the night of the 31/10/1917, a working party of 15 R.E., 15 Attached Infantry and two shifts of 45 Infantry, were used to straighten out the debris at the bottom of the gap, preparatory to filling in with sandbags.

A Dam was commenced to fill up the breach, but this did not reach sufficient height to cope with the rapidly rising tide; also the work was interfered with by shell fire, the following casualties being caused :-

    R.E. 3 Wounded.
    Infantry 7 wounded.

For the night of the 1/2nd instant, the following working parties were organised :-

		East Bank		West Bank		Time.
		Off.	O.R.	Off.	O.R.	
R.E.	1st shift.	1	6	1	6	5-30p.m/11-30p.m
Attd. Infantry.	1st shift.	1	11	1	6	do.
R.E.	2nd shift.	1	6	1	6	11-30p.m/5-30 a.m.
Infantry	1st shift.	1	45	1	45	5-30p.m.-9-30p.m.
do.	2nd shift.	1	35	1	35	9-30p.m.-1/30a.m.
do.	3rd shift.	1	20	1	20	1-30a.m./5-30 a.m
Cyclists	1st shift.	-	50	-	-	6 p.m.to 11 p.m.
Cyclists	2nd shift.	-	50	-	-	11 p.m.to 2 a.m.

From each bank the R.E. were employed laying the bags, supervising the filling of the bags, and the chain of sandbag carriers; the infantry party were employed on each bank, half filling sandbags,

- 2 -

and half forming a carrying chain on to the Dam.   The cyclists were entirely employed on carrying sandbags filled with bricks, from a dump of same, situated near VAUXHALL BRIDGE, NIEUPORT.

No. 3 Results.

A sandbag dam was constructed, 12 feet wide at the base, tapering to 6 feet wide at the top, the height being about 7 to 8 feet.   The centre of the Dam was partially filled with brick in sandbags.

The structure had reached the correct height at about 11-30 p.m.; the remainder of the time was used in thickening the toe of the Dam on the North side, by throwing in sandbags filled with brick, and a few with earth.

Work was stopped at 3-30 a.m.

4. / Throughout the first relief the enemy was using a single gun against the dam and its vicinity with two bursts of fire about 8-30 p.m. and 10-30 p.m. At intervals and occasional bursts of machine gun fire.   During this period one man was wounded.

At 12-45 a.m. however, and every 15 minutes until 3-30 a.m. salvos were sent bursting directly over the dam and especially on the West bank.   The total casualties were

R.E.	1 O.R. killed.	3 O.R. wounded.
Inf. & Cyclists.	1 O.R. killled	4 O.R. wounded.

5. Working Parties.

The working parties supplied by the 6th and 7th Battalions Manchester Regt. did especially good work on this job, especially the first shifts on each bank.

(Sgd.) J. H. MOUSLEY,

Major,
O.C. 427 Field Co. R.E.

4/11/1917.

Secret.   Copy No. 13

C.R.E., 42nd (East Lancs.) Division, (Warning) Order No. 28.

- By -

LIEUT. COLONEL D. S. MACINNES, C.M.G., D.S.O., R.E.

Mr. B

14th Novr., 1917.

1. In connection with the **relief of the 42nd Division** that is taking place between 17th and 21st instant, units attached to the 42nd Divisional R.E. will cease work as follows :-

    63rd Field Co. R.E.   On morning of 16th instant.

    100 attached infantry (9th Division) on morning of 16th instant.

    13th Corps Cyclist Battalion.   (Not known. Will be notified later).

    'A' Coy. 9th Batt. Seaforth Highlanders (Pioneers)   On morning of 16th instant.

2. Units of the 42nd Divisional R.E. will be relieved by incoming units as follows :-

    427 Field Co. R.E.)
    428 Field Co. R.E.)   On night of 18th/19th instant.

    429 Field Co. R.E.   On night of 19th/20th instant, but may be delayed until night of 20th/21st.

3. Infantry working parties at present being supplied will cease as follows :-

    50 O.R. found by Reserve Infantry Brigade for Wellington Camp.   On evening of 15th instant.

    Two parties 50 O.R. each found by Reserve Infantry Brigade for Eastern and Western Switches.   On evening of 15th instant.

    20 O.R. found by Reserve Infantry Brigade for Pioneer Company for road work.   On evening of 15th instant. ~~(If necessary 20 cyclists will be found for this work on evening of 15th)~~.

4. No more stores will be sent up to the forward area for Units after the following nights :-

    63rd Field Co. R.E.   After night of 15th/16th.

    'A' Coy. 9th Batt. Seaforth Highlanders (Pioneers).   After night of 15th/16th.

    427 Field Co. R.E.)
    428 Field Co. R.E.)   After night of 16th/17th.
    429 Field Co. R.E.)

    <u>Note.</u>   For stores urgently required by 429 Field Co. R.E. for night of 17th/18th special arrangements will be made.

- 2 -

5. The dismounted portions of 427 and 428 Field Companies R.E. will probably be required to proceed by barge from TULPEN on the night of 18th/19th instant, their transport proceeding by march route on the morning of the 19th instant.

The 429 Field Co. R.E. will probably proceed by barge from TULPEN on the night of the 19th/20th (or possibly on the night of the 20th/21st), its transport leaving on the following morning.

6. The Infantry attached to the Field Companies will probably move with them and remain with them throughout the move.

7. R.E. Stores. Company Commanders in charge of Forward R.E. Dumps will send to this office stock lists of stores in those dumps including main dumps of reserve bridging material and explosives, made up to the night of 15th/16th instant.

Further instructions will be issued as to the actual handing over of R.E. Stores to incoming units.

Capt. & Adjt. R.E.,
42nd Divisional R.E.

Copies to :-

1. 427 Field Co. R.E.
2. 428 Field Co. R.E.
3. 429 Field Co. R.E.
4. 63rd Field Co. R.E.
5. 'A' Coy., 9th Seaforth Highlanders (Pioneers).
6. ~~13th Corps Cyclists Battalion.~~
7. 'C', 42nd Division.
8. ~~H.Q., 125th Brigade.~~
9. ~~H.Q., 126th Brigade.~~
10. ~~H.Q., 127th Brigade.~~
11. ~~'C', 9th Division.~~
12. C.R.E., 9th Division.
13. War Diary.
14. File.
15. Spare.

SECRET.   Copy No...9..

C.R.E., 42nd (East Lancs.) Division, Order No. 29.

- by -

LIEUT. COLONEL D.S. MACINNES, C.M.G., D.S.O., R.E.

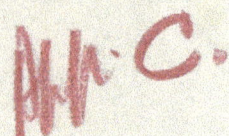

15th November, 1917.

1. The XVth Corps is being relieved by the XXXVI French Corps, commencing 18th November; the relief of the front line taking place on the nights of 17th/18th and 18th/19th November, 1917.

2. The 42nd Division is being relieved by the 133rd French Division, and is moving out of the XVth Corps Area to the First Army Area via WORMHOUDT.

3. Relief of the 42nd Divisional R.E. will takeplace on the night 18th/19th November in accordance with the attached March Table.

4. The detail of working parties and the dates on which they will rejoin their units is shown in attached table.

5. The 100 infantry attached to each Field Company R.E. will move with the Field Company.

6. All defence schemes, trench and local area maps, air photos, details of work in hand or projected will be handed over on relief.

7. One officer per Field Co. R.E. will be left with the relieving units for 24 hours after the relief of the Field Company concerned is complete. Arrangements for these officers rejoining their units will be notified later.

8. Progress of all reliefs and completion of all moves will be reported by wire to Headquarters Divisional R.E.

9. Command of the 42nd Divisional Front is passing to the G.O.C., 133rd French Division at 10-0 a.m., 19th November.
    Headquarters 42nd Division will close at COXYDE BAINS at 10-0 a.m. 19th November, and re-open in the WORMHOUDT Area at a place and time to be notified later.
    On 20th November, 42nd Divisional Headquarters will move to WALLON CAPPEL; time and place will be notified as soon as possible.

10. Headquarters, 42nd Divisional R.E. will move with Headquarters 42nd Division.

11. Acknowledge.

                                            Capt. & Adjt. R.E.,
                                            42nd Divisional R.E.

Distribution :-

        Copy 1. 427 Field Co. R.E.
             2. 428 Field Co. R.E.
             3. 429 Field Co. R.E.
             4. 'Q', 42nd Division.
             5. 'Q', 42nd Division.
             6. H.Q. 125 Brigade.
             7. H.Q. 126 Brigade.
             8. H.Q. 127 Brigade.
             9. War Diary.
            10. File.
            11. Spare.

March Table to accompany C.R.E., 42nd Division Order No. 29.

Date	Formation	From	To	Remarks.
Night 18/19th.	428 Field Co. R.E.	Line	Horse Lines.	On relief by French.
19th.	428 Field Co. R.E.	Horse Lines	WORMHOUDT Area A.	To move under orders of G.O.C. 125 Inf. Brigade. Personnel to march to ADINKERKE where they will embark at 9-0 a.m. to BERGUES, whence they march to rejoin their Brigade Group. Transport to march via FURNES - HONDSCHOOTE - WYLDER, to be South of COXYDE - LA PANNE road by 8-0 a.m.
20th.	428 Field Co. R.E.	WORMHOUDT Area A.	WORMHOUDT Area B.	Under orders of G.O.C. 126th Infantry Brigade.
21st.	428 Field Co. R.E.	WORMHOUDT Area B.	WALLON CAPPEL.	ditto.
22nd.	428 Field Co. R.E.	WALLON CAPPEL.	First Army Area.	ditto.
Night 18th/19th.	427 Field Co. R.E.	Line.	OOST DUNKERKE & COXYDE AREA.	On relief by French. To come under orders of G.O.C. 125 Infantry Brigade from 12 noon 18th inst.
19th.	427 Field Co. R.E.	OOST DUNKERKE & COXYDE AREA.	TETEGHEM.	Under orders of G.O.C. 125th Infantry Brigade.
20th.	427 Field Co. R.E.	TETEGHEM.	WORMHOUDT Area A.	ditto.
21st.	427 Field Co. R.E.	WORMHOUDT Area A.	WORMHOUDT Area B.	ditto.
22nd.	427 Field Co. R.E.	WORMHOUDT Area B.	WALLON CAPPEL	ditto.
23rd.	427 Field Co. R.E.	WALLON CAPPEL	First Army Area.	ditto.
Night 19th/20th).	429 Field Co. R.E.	Line	Horse Lines.	Further orders will be issued later regarding subsequent moves.

Working Party Table to accompany C.R.E. 42nd Division Order No. 29.

Strength	By Whom Supplied.	Locality of Work.	Hours of Work and for whom working.	Hour and date on which party will rejoin unit.	Remarks.
50 Other Ranks.	127th Inf. Brigade.	WELLINGTON CAMP.	8-0 a.m. to 4-0 p.m. 63rd Field Co. R.E.	4 p.m. 15/11/17.	
50 Other Ranks.	do.	Advanced Bde. H.Q. BRICUETERIE.	Attached 126 Inf. Bde. work under 428 Fld.Co.R.E.	2 p.m. 15/11/17.	To be relieved by 126 Inf. Brigade.
2 Officers and 100 O.R.	do.	Eastern & Western Switches.	8-30 a.m. to 2-30 p.m. 427 Field Co. R.E.	After work, 15/11/17.	
13 Other Ranks.	do.	Making Horse Lines.	9 a.m. to 3 p.m. 428th Field Co. R.E.	3 p.m. 15/11/17.	
50 Other Ranks.	126th Inf. Brigade.	GLASGOW DUMP.	8-30 a.m. to 4-30 p.m. Loading R.E. Stores.	4-30 p.m. 17/11/17.	
200 Other Ranks.	XIII Corps Cyclists.	NIEUPORT.	Nightly under C.F.E.		Continue work until night 18th/19th Nov, and available on that night for urgent work only.

SECRET.

Copy No. 11.

C.R.E., 42nd (E. Lancs.) Division, Order No. 30.

- by -

LT. COLONEL A. N. LANFORD, R.E.

25/11/1917.

Reference 1/40,000 Sheet 36a.
1/10,000 Sheet 36 S.E.3 (Secret).
1/10,000 Sheet 36c. N.E. 1 (Secret).

1. The 42nd Division is relieving the 25th Division in the GIVENCHY and Canal Sectors on the 27th and 28th instant.

2. On the right the CAMBRIN Sector is held by the 74th Infantry Brigade, 25th Division, which at 6-0 a.m. 29th instant will come under the orders of 1st Corps (46th Division).

On the left the front is held by the 1st Portuguese Division.

The Southern Divisional Boundary will be as follows :-
From the front line at A.27.b.8.4 - Along Boyau '15' to BACK STREET - Along BACK STREET to BURBURE ALLEY - BURBURE ALLEY to its junction with WIMPOLE STREET (All inclusive to 42nd Division) - A.19.d.10.00 on the BETHUNE - LA BASSEE Road - Along and South of the BETHUNE - LA BASSEE Road to join the existing Corps Boundary in F.20.a. and thence through F.18.a.8.5. to F.11.a.0.0.

3. (a). The 125th and 127th Inf. Brigades are relieving the 75th and 7th Infantry Brigades in the Canal and GIVENCHY Sectors on the 28th and 27th instants respectively.

(b) The 126th Inf. Brigade will be in Divisional Reserve in the BETHUNE Area.

(c) The 127th and 125th Machine Gun Companies are relieving the Machine Gun Companies of 25th Division in the GIVENCHY and Canal Sectors on the 28th and 29th instants respectively, ie. 24 hours after the Infantry have gone into the line.

4. Command of the 25th Divisional Front (Canal and GIVENCHY Sectors) is passing to the G.O.C. 42nd Division at 12 noon on the 29th instant.

5. The move of the 42nd Divisional R.E. will take place in

- 2 -

accordance with the attached March Table.

6. Field Companies R.E. 42nd Division will march to the new area with the Infantry Brigade to which they are affiliated.

427 and 429 Field Companies R.E. will relieve Field Companies R.E. in the Canal and GIVENCHY Sectors under arrangements that will be notified later. The 428th Field Co. R.E. will be in Divisional Reserve.

7. Headquarters R.E. 42nd Division will close at AIRE at 8-0 a.m. on 29th instant and open at LOCON at 12 noon the same day.

8. Progress of moves and reliefs will be reported daily to this office.

                                           Capt. & Adjt. R.E.,
                                    for C.R.E., 42nd Division.

25/11/1917.

Distribution :-

    Normal, plus :-

        125 Brigade.
        126 Brigade.
        127 Brigade.
        'Q' 42nd Division.

- MARCH TABLE for 42nd Divisional R.E. -

Date	Formation.	From	To	Remarks.
26 November.	429 Field Co. R.E.	LAMBRES-ISBERGUES Area.	OBLINGHEM - MT.BERNENCHON-HAMEL-ESSARS-portion of BETHUNE Area.	To march under orders of G.O.C. 127th Brigade.
27 November.	429 Field Co. R.E.	OBLINGHEM-BETHUNE Area.	Line.	The Field Co. of 25th Divl. R.E. relieved and all details will be notified later.
27 November	427 Field Co. R.E.	THIENNES Area.	OBLINGHEM-BETHUNE Area.	To march under orders of G.O.C. 125th Inf. Brigade.
28th Novr.	427 Field Co. R.E.	OBLINGHEM-BETHUNE Area.	Line.	Field Co. of 25th Divl. R.E. relieved and all details will be notified later.
27th Novr.	428 Field Co. R.E.	ROCQUETOIRE Area.	LAMBRES-ISBERGUES-ROBECQ Area.	To march under orders of G.O.C. 126th Inf. Brigade.
28th Novr.	428 Field Co. R.E.	LAMBRES-ISBERGUES Area.	Divisional Reserve in OBLINGHEM-BETHUNE Area.	To march under orders of G.O.C. 126th Inf. Brigade.

SECRET.

H.Q.,
42ND (E.L.) DIVISION,
R.E.
No. C2/216.
Date. 25.11.17.

O.C. 427 Field Co. R.E.
O.C. 428 Field Co. R.E.
O.C. 429 Field Co. R.E.

App.E

Reference Map. BETHUNE, 1/40,000.

With reference to C.R.E., 42nd (East Lancs.) Division Order No. 32 of today:-

1. 429 Field Co. R.E. will relieve 135th Field Co. R.E. on 27th instant, relief to be completed by 8-0 p.m. 135th Field Co. R.E. Headquarters are at SHAFT SENTRY, F.3.c.4.3. and the relief can be carried out by daylight.

427 Field Co. R.E. will relieve 106th Field Co. R.E. on 28th instant, relief to be completed by 8-0 p.m. 106th Field Co. R.E. Headquarters are at LE PREOL, F.15.b.7.5. and the relief can be carried out by daylight.

428th Field Co. R.E. (less 1 section) will remain in reserve area. One section 428th Field Co. R.E. will take over the workshops at F.3.c.7... by 12 noon on 29th instant.

2. Advance parties will be sent as follows :-
429th Field Co. R.E.   1 Officer, 1 representative from each section, together with 2 storemen and a suitable sapper to take over the running of a water point.

To proceed on 26th instant by arrangement with 127th Inf. Brigade if possible, and if not, on bicycles, to report to O.C. 135th Field Co. at SHAFT SENTRY, F.3.c.4.3.

427th Field Co. R.E.   1 Officer, 1 representative from each section and 2 storemen.

To proceed on 27th instant by arrangement with Brigade if possible and if not, on bicycles, to report to O.C. 106th Field Co. R.E. at LE PREOL, F.15.b.7.5.

Both parties to take sufficient rations to cover period until their respective Field Companies arrive.

3. The Tramway Party (1 R.E. officer found by 428 Field Co. R.E. and 12 O.R. found by Infantry Brigades) will be rationed by 429 Field Co. R.E. from 25th instant inclusive and will be taken on ration strength accordingly.

4. The Divisional R.E. Dump is at F.3.c.5.3. (approx.). Each Field Co. R.E. will send 1 sapper as issuer to report to R.S.M. Sowray at the Dump as soon as possible after arrival in new area.
Sappers who have had experience in this work should be sent.

O.C. 428 Fd Cy RE. will also send a Clerk to report to R.S.M. Sowray at the Dump.

A.N. Walker.
Capt. & Adjt. R.E.,
for C.R.E., 42nd Division.

25/11/17.

Copies to :-
'G', 42nd Division.
B... 125 Brigade.
B... 126 Brigade.
B... 127 Brigade.

Vol. 11

WAR DIARY

of

Hdqrs. R.E. 42nd (E.L.) Division

from 1st to 31st December 1917.

(Volume 4)

Confidential
ORIGINAL

Army Form C. 2118.

WAR DIARY
INTELLIGENCE SUMMARY
(Erase heading not required.)

Reference Maps.
France. Sheets 36A.SE; 36.S.W.
36.B.NE; 36.a.M.W.
Scale 1:40,000

Instructions regarding War Diaries and Intelligence Summaries are contained in F.S. Regs., Part II. and the Staff Manual respectively. Title pages will be prepared in manuscript.

Place	Date	Hour	Summary of Events and Information	Remarks and references to Appendices
LOCON.	1-12-17 to 21-12-17		H.Q. R.E. employed in organisation of R.E. work in GIVENCHY and CAMBRIN Sectors. Two field companies in the line and one in reserve. The nature of work was maintenance of trenches (revetting, drainage and provision of shell proof accommodation in and East of FESTUBERT Rd and HARLEY Street. Very little shell proof accommodation existed and the Divisional R.E. were ordered to concentrate on this work as a precaution against possible enemy activity. The trench tramway system was maintained and repairs. The enemy was chiefly quiet throughout this period.	/MM/
	22-12-17		Lt.Col. J.T. MacINNES C.M.G. D.S.O. R.E. left the Divisional R.E. to assume the appointment of Inspector of Mines, G.H.Q. Lt.Col R. PRATT, D.S.O. R.E., took over the work of C.R.E. of the Division.	/MM/
	23-12-17 to 28-12-17		Work carried on as above, but all concreting work held up owing to continuous frost.	/MM/
	29-12-17		422 field Coy R.E. and 14 Batt. S. Lancs Rg. Pioneers joined the R.E. for work allotted to them.	/MM/
	30-12-17		Above companies employed in taking over work allotted to them.	/MM/
	31-12-17		Commenced work. Frost continued and much work held up.	/MM/

A.N. Walker.
Captn.
Adjt. H.Q. R.E. to CRE
46th Div.

D.A.G.,
   3rd Echelon,
     B.E.F.

      Reference G.S.18/18 of 9/4/17.

      Herewith War Diary of 427th Field Company R.E.,
for March 1917.

      Please acknowledge receipt.

10/4/17

                              Captain,
                         for Major General,
                    Commanding 42nd Division.

Vol 1².

WAR DIARY

of

Negro. R.E., 42nd (E. Lanc.) Division

from 1st to 31st January 1918

(Volume 5)

Confidential
Original

Army Form C. 2118.

WAR DIARY
INTELLIGENCE SUMMARY.

Reference Map.
FRANCE. BETHUNE. 36A. SE 36 SW } Scale
Corrected Sheet. 36.B. NE 36cNW } 1:40,000.

(Erase heading not required.)

Instructions regarding War Diaries and Intelligence Summaries are contained in F. S. Regs., Part II. and the Staff Manual respectively. Title pages will be prepared in manuscript.

Place	Date	Hour	Summary of Events and Information	Remarks and references to Appendices
LOCON.	1-1-18 to 23-1-18		42nd Divl. RE, together with 1 Field Co. RE and Pionier Batt. of 55th Division still in the GIVENCHY – CANAL Sector. The principal works in hand were the provision of shell proof accommodation in and in front of the VILLAGE LINE and the wiring of the VILLAGE LINE front-in. The early part of the month severely hampered the progress of concrete work and the consequent thaw precautions upset the transport of R.E. materials forward. The trench tramway system was developed and additional lines put down to supply R.A. and T.M. batteries with ammunition.	MW
	24-1-18.		The 472 nd (West Lancs) Field Co, R.E. was relieved by the 423rd (West Lancs) Field Co, R.E.	MW
	25-1-18 to 31-1-18.		Work carried on as above. A severe shortage of R.E. materials, especially of cement, caused a reorganisation of work and heavy rains about the 16th and 17th instants resulted in much work on trench maintenance and drainage, being carried out up to the end of the month.	MW

J. Norman Walker
Capt & Adjt
for Lieut-Col
CRE 42 Divn

S.A 13

WAR DIARY.
of
Hdqrs 42nd (E. Lancs) Divisional R.E.
from 1st to 28th February 1918

(Volume 5)

Confidential
ORIGINAL

Army Form C. 2118.

WAR DIARY
INTELLIGENCE SUMMARY.

Reference Map.
BETHUNE, Contrived Sheet.
1/40,000.

(Erase heading not required.)

Place	Date	Hour	Summary of Events and Information	Remarks and references to Appendices
LOCON	1-2-18 to 12-2-18.		42nd Divisional R.E. in GIVENCHY - CANAL Sector. Work chiefly on provision of Shell proof shelters in front and Reserve lines. Work much hampered by lack of cement and general shortage of R.E. materials. Specially urgent wiring work was done on the VILLAGE LINE in FESTUBERT and CAMBRIN Regions, and much trench maintenance and improvements in latter region. Preparations were made for forthcoming handing over to the 55th Division.	MW
	13.2.18.		The 419th Fd. Coy R.E. relieved by the 419th (West Lancs) Field Coy R.E. and marched to LES HARISOIRS, (W26.84).	See App. MM A.
	14.2.18.		427th Fd. Coy. R.E. handed over work to 422nd (West Lancs) Field Co R.E. and marched to BUSNES. 428 & 423rd Cos. R.E. remained at LE QUESNOY, handing over work to 423rd Fd Co R.E. MM
	15.2.18.		Hdqrs R.E. moved to HINGES. W.16.a.0.8.	MM
HINGES	16.2.18.		429 Fd. Co. commenced work along with an Infantry Battalion on the HOUCHIN- LOCON line, wiring with double apron fence, under 1st Corps orders.	MM
	17.2.18.		427 Fd. Co. moved from BUSNES to BEUVRY (F.14.c.6.8) to come under orders of CRE. 55th Division for work on VILLAGE LINE. 428th Fd. Co. came under orders of 1st Corps for work on mined dugouts in CAMBRIN region. The 17th Batt. Northumberland Fusiliers (Pioneers) arrived about this time & was attached to the 42nd Division as its Pioneer Battalion.	MM

WAR DIARY
—OF—
INTELLIGENCE SUMMARY.
(Erase heading not required.)

Army Form C. 2118.

Reference Map.
BETHUNE. Combined Sheet. 1/40,000.

Place	Date	Hour	Summary of Events and Information	Remarks and references to Appendices
HINGES.	20.2.18		479 Fd Coy. moved from LES HARISOIRS to HINGES (N.15.b.1.9) and took on additional wiring work on ESSARS locality. A reconnaissance was also made about this line of the suitable sites for S. pontoon bridges over the LA BASSEE Canal to facilitate transferring of troops from one side of the canal to the other in case of attack. This work was taken in hand by the 479 Fd Coy, using the pontoon equipment of two Divisions in the line.	/MM
	21-2-18 to 26-2-18.		The 478 & Fd Coy's horses were severely attacked by Mange about 75% being evacuated. 479 Fd Coy had also many cases All possible steps were taken to overcome this disease.	/MM
			Arrivals. Lieut T. F. HALE. Medical Corps United States Reserve.	
	19-2-18			

J. Newman Waller
Capt & Adjutant
(for furnished Divn
C.R.E. 40th Divn)

SECRET.   **App A**   Copy No. 12

C.R.E., 42nd (East Lancs.) Division Order No. 34.

- by -

LIEUT. COLONEL R.E.B. PRATT, D.S.O., R.E.

Reference Map: 1/40,000.
BETHUNE Combined Sheet.   10th February, 1918.

----

1. The 42nd Division is being relieved in the Line by the 55th Division commencing 12th February.

2. On relief, the 42nd Division is moving into the BUSHES - BURBURE - FOUQUIERES Training Area, where it will come into G.H.Q. Reserve at 6 p.m., 14th February.

3. Command of the 42nd Division Front (Canal and Givenchy Sectors) is passing to G.O.C., 55th Division at 10 a.m. 15th February.

4. The relief of the 42nd Divisional R.E. by the 55th Divisional R.E. will take place as follows, moves being in accordance with the attached March Table :-
   (a) The 428th Field Coy. R.E. will remain in their present billets but will arrange mutually with O.C. 423 Field Coy. R.E. (at present at LE PREOL) for the handing over of the work in the right forward sector to 423 Field Coy. R.E. by the 14th instant.
   (b) The 429th Field Coy. R.E. will be relieved by the 419th Field Coy. R.E. on the 13th instant and will take over the billets at LES HARISOIRS (W.2) at present occupied by the 419 Field Coy. R.E.
   O.C. 429 Field Coy. R.E. will send an advance party of one officer and 4 N.C.Os. to report to O.C. 419 Field Coy. R.E. at LES HARISOIRS on the afternoon 11th instant to take over work of wiring of the HOUCHIN-LOCON Line.
   O.C. 419th Field Coy. R.E. is sending an advance party of two officers and 4 N.C.Os. on the 11th instant to report to O.C. 429th Field Coy. R.E. to take over work in left forward sector.
   (c) The 427th Field Coy. R.E. will be relieved by the 422nd Field Coy. R.E. on the 14th instant and will march under the orders of the Brig. General Commanding 126th Inf. Brigade. Arrangements will be made by O.C. 427th Field Coy. R.E. with the 126th Brigade as to advance party to be sent.
   O.C. 422 Field Coy. R.E. is sending an advance party of two officers and 4 N.C.Os. on the afternoon 12th instant to report to O.C. 427 Field Coy. R.E. to take over work on right of reserve area.
   (d) 423 Field Coy. R.E. will remain in their present billets and will hand over to the advance party of the 422 Field Coy. R.E. (mentioned in sub-para. (c)) the work on left of reserve area. The attached Infantry of the 423 Field Coy. R.E. on arrival will be billetted in the billets at present occupied by the attached infantry of the 428 Field Coy. R.E.

5. The Tramway Officer and Party of 23 O.R. will be relieved on 13th instant. The Tramway Officer of 55th Division will inspect the line on the 12th instant under arrangements to be made mutually between this officer and Lieut. W.L. Mellor, M.C., 427th Field Co. R.E.

6. The Infantry attached to the Field Companies R.E. will return to their respective units on the 11th instant, taking rations for the 11th and 12th instant.

7. The Reserve Brigade will cease to find working parties after 4 p.m. on the 11th instant.

8. All trench and area stores, plans, Defence Schemes, air photos, etc. will be handed over and receipts obtained. The regular series of maps will not be handed over but will be dealt with in accordance with instructions previously issued.

9. Progress of moves and reliefs will be reported daily to this office at 6 p.m.

10. Administrative Instructions will be issued separately.

11. C.R.E's Office will close at LOCON and re-open at HINGES at 10 a.m. on the 15th instant.

12. ACKNOWLEDGE.

Capt. & Adjt.,
42nd Divisional R.E.

Issued by   D.R.   at   p.m. 10/2/1918.
            Orderly.

Distribution:-

Copy No. 1. 427 Field Coy. R.E.
         2. 428 Field Coy. R.E.
         3. 429 Field Coy. R.E.
         4. 423 Field Coy. R.E.
         5. 'G', 42nd Division.
         6. 'Q', 42nd Division.
7, 8 and 9. 126, 125 and 127 Inf. Brigades.
        10. S.S.O., 42nd Division.
        11. C.R.E., 55th Division.
12 and 13. War Diary.
        14. File.

March Table to Accompany C.R.E's Order No. 34.

Serial No.	Date.	Unit.	From	To	In relief of.	Route & Remarks.
1.	Feb. 13th.	429 Field Coy. R.E.	Pont. CORBE.	LES HARISOIRE.	419 Field Coy. R.E.	By most direct route. O.C. 429 Field Coy. R.E. to arrange time and route in conjunction with 126/2/5 as not to clash with 126 Bde. move into DIV. Reserve Area.
2.	Feb. 14th.	427 Field Coy. R.E.	LE PHEOL.	BURNES.	-	To march under orders of Brig. General Commanding 126 Infantry Brigade.

42nd Divisional Engineers.

C. R. E.

42nd EAST LANCS DIVISION

MARCH 1918

Vol 14

WAR DIARY
of
Hqrs. R.E. 42nd (E.L.) Division
from 1st to 31st March 1918.

(Volume 5).

Consulted
ORIGINAL

Army Form C. 2118.

WAR DIARY
INTELLIGENCE SUMMARY.
(Erase heading not required.)

Reference maps:—
Bethune Contoured Sheet. 1:40,000
Lens Sheet II. 1:100,000
Bauce Sheet 57D 1:40,000

Place	Date	Hour	Summary of Events and Information	Remarks and references to Appendices
HINGES	1/3/18 to 3/3/18		407 Fld Coy at BEUVRY working on VILLAGE LINE under orders of 55th Division. 408 Fld Coy R.E. at LE QUESNOY working direct under 1st Corps on provision of dugout accommodation in forward area. 429 Fld Coy R.E. at HINGES working under 1st Corps on wiring of Western sector of HOUCHIN – LOCON line and of bridgeheads in LESTREM area and in construction of trenches in the HOUCHIN-LOCON line.	
	4/3/18		407 Fld Coy moved to BUSNES for training. Major General G. Solly-Flood, QMG, A.S.O., G.O.C. 42nd Divn addressed the Officers and NCOs of the Divisional R.E. setting forth briefly the present situation in France & the aims of the Division whilst in training	Null Null
	5/3/18		H.Q.R.E. moved to LA BEUVRIERE	Null
LA BEUVRIERE	6/3/18 – 21/3/18		428 and 429 Fld Coys continued works as above. 407 Fld Coy employed on training laying particular stress on smartening up the men and improving their fighting qualities by means of bayonet fighting and musketry training. During this period the Division had to be prepared to move primarily at 48 hours notice, then at 24 hours notice, and finally at 12 hours notice, either to reinforce immediate front, Portuguese Corps or elsewhere in France. Precautionary orders were issued to Field Coys and administrative details arranged.	Null
	22/3/18		A warning order for a move to following day was received in the afternoon, and definite orders	

Army Form C. 2118.

WAR DIARY
or
INTELLIGENCE SUMMARY.
(Erase heading not required.)

Place	Date	Hour	Summary of Events and Information	Remarks and references to Appendices
			about 1.30 a.m. were received instructions for Bn to move by bus to BASSEUX Area or even further South	MW
	23/3/18		427 & 428 Fd Coys embussed on BUSNES - LILLERS Road at 10:30 a.m, the latter Company having a long distance to cover to the embussing point. HQRE & 419 Fd Cy embussed on the WESTISNEUL - LA BOISSIERE Road at 10:30 a.m. Transport proceeded by road to MORCHY BRETON. 419 Fd Cy was bivouaced to the right of AYETTE, HdQrs RE 427 & 428 Fd Coys RE at ADINFER, & were kept in readiness to move forward if situation demanded.	MW
ADINFER	24/3/18		HdQrs RE moved early to MONCHY au BOIS. In afternoon the Fd Coys were ordered to hold themselves in readiness to proceed to vicinity of LOGEAST WOOD and later orders were issued for 427 & 419 Fd Coys to move forward to take over work on Fifth System and occupy if necessary the old German line BEHAGNIES - ERVILLERS. Owing to failure of 419 Bn own to guides to arrive at rendez-vous notified by Div HQ, this unit was not reached. 428 Fd Cy was ordered late at night to act as infantry escort to guns and moved from ADINFER about 2:30 a.m. The transport of the 419 RE arrived after an unsatisfactory journey, not having drawn rations for day of arrival.	MW
MONCHY au BOIS	25/3/18		427 & 419 Fd Coys together with Pioneer Battalion took up position on railway embankment immediately North of ACHIET LE GRAND. In conjunction with general retirement of the	

WAR DIARY
INTELLIGENCE SUMMARY

Army Form C. 2118.

(Erase heading not required.)

Instructions regarding War Diaries and Intelligence Summaries are contained in F. S. Regs., Part II. and the Staff Manual respectively. Title pages will be prepared in manuscript.

Place	Date	Hour	Summary of Events and Information	Remarks and references to Appendices
			Division Field Coys and Pioneer Battalion were ordered in the evening to fall back in	
			4 bounds finally taking up a position in the vicinity of ESSARTS LES BUCQUOY. Magic	
			R.E. moved in afternoon to FONQUEVILLERS.	MW
FONQUEVILLERS	26/3/18		In afternoon Fd Coys and Pioneer Batt.ⁿ were ordered to concentrate at a Divisional Reserve	
			under the C.R.E. in the vicinity of ESSARTS and a report centre was opened at the Crossroads	MW
			HANNESCAMPS to maintain communication with C.R.E's Office.	
	27/3/18		Field Coys and Pioneer Batt.ⁿ distributed to Infty Bdes for work under Brigade orders	
		7.30 pm	About 7.30 pm orders received to form ½ a Coy, Pioneer Batt.ⁿ and a Composite Batt.ⁿ of details	MW
			into a Divisional Reserve under the C.R.E. Orders were modified about immediately and Pioneers	MW
			were put under orders of 125 Infty Bde.	
	28/3/18		Adqrs R.E. moved at very short notice to ST AMAND. Fd Coys were again put under Brigade	MW
			orders as fighting troops and ordered to rest, but moved forward into position straight away	
ST AMAND	29/3/18		In afternoon orders received for relief of Division by 41st Division. 2nd Coy Pioneer Batt.ⁿ	MW
			received orders to move to vicinity of GOMMECOURT WOOD to work on	
			PURPLE LINE	
	30/3/18		Reconnaissance made by C.R.E. accompanied by a G.S. officer, of suitable positions for	

INTELLIGENCE SUMMARY
or
WAR DIARY

Army Form C. 2118.

(Erase heading not required.)

Place	Date	Hour	Summary of Events and Information	Remarks and references to Appendices
	31/3/18		Strong points in the PURPLE LINE Orders issued to No Coys to commence work forthwith. One Coy of Pioneers attached to 727 Fd Coy for work on Strong point in extreme night.	AMN
			Similar work would have been carried out at night as for previous night with addition of renewing 2 Coys of Pioneers which were given to 727 Bde for wiring work, but orders were received for relief of 41st Division by 42nd Division, and Field Coys were placed at the disposal of Infty Bdes and Pioneer Battalion at disposal of 125 Infty Bde.	MW
	23/18			
			Casualties up to 31/3/18 427 Fd. Coy RE: 3 OR wounded	
			428 — 2 OR killed 1 wounded	
			429 — 3 OR wounded	

Walker
A. Norman
Capt RE
for CRE 42nd Division

IV.Corps.
Third Army.

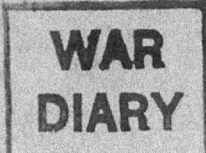

Headquarters,

ROYAL ENGINEERS, 42nd Division.

A P R I L

1 9 1 8

WAR DIARY
or
INTELLIGENCE SUMMARY.

Vol 15

Original

WAR DIARY.
Headquarters 42nd Division RE
from 1st to 30th April 1918

WAR DIARY / INTELLIGENCE SUMMARY

Army Form C. 2118.

(Erase heading not required.)

Reference map: France 57.D. 1:40,000

Place	Date	Hour	Summary of Events and Information	Remarks and references to Appendices
ST AMAND	1/4/18		To enable work to be done on the Purple Line, 2 Officers and 18 OR were withdrawn from Field Coys working under Brigade Orders.	Appx
	2/4/18		Transfert of all field Coys moved from Coun to Souastre. Fd. Coys put under orders of 126 Bdes to which infantry affiliated i.e. 427 Coy to 125 Bde, 428 Coy to 126 Bde, 429 Coy to 127 Bde and one Coy of Pioneer Batt" was given to each Infty Bde.	Appx
	3/4/18		H.Q. 429 RE moved to HENU. Road from HANNESCAMPS to ESSARTS reported to be becoming badly damaged. Consequently a Reconnaissance was made of an old Decauville Line running from ESSARTS to MONCHY au BOIS - BIENVILLERS road. Subsequently decided not to use same. Party of Reserve	Appx
HENU	4/4/18		Divisions of work watching and repair of roads becoming serious. roads of Pioneer Batt" ordered to look on SOUASTRE - BONQUEVILLERS road.	Appx
	5/4/18		Work on roads commenced, SOUASTRE - ST AMAND, GOMMECOURT - ESSARTS, SOUASTRE - FONQUEVILLERS. WPs found from Reserve details and reinforcements of Infty Bdes. One Section fur Fd Coy recalled from line for work on roads and water supply. A water and roads officer instituted.	Appx
	6/4/18		Continuance of heavy rain making roads in bad state. Additional work on BIENVILLERS - ESSARTS road commenced. Orders received for relief of Division by 62nd Division. Orders and	Appx

Army Form C. 2118.

WAR DIARY
or
INTELLIGENCE SUMMARY.
(Erase heading not required.)

Place	Date	Hour	Summary of Events and Information	Remarks and references to Appendices
	7/4/18		Administrative instructions issued at 11 p.m. to Fd. Coys.	
			Major's RE handed over to 62nd Division and moved to PAS. At 7.30 a.m. sudden orders were received for 427 Fd. Coy. to move out of the line forthwith instead of on following night. Material	
			RE proceeded immediately & found accommodation in HENU and then waited for Company	a.m.
			at SOUASTRE and guided them to HENU. Company very tired.	
PAS.	8/4/18		427 Fd. Coy. wired by lorry and transport by road to VAUCHELLES. 428 Fd. Coy.	
			came out of line at night and moved by lorry to PAS, transport moving by road in the	
			afternoon. 429 Fd. Coy. RE came out of line and proceeded by march route to HENU, transport	p.m.
			reaching there earlier in afternoon.	
	9/4/18		Field Companies employed on cleaning up, sorting and checking equipment.	p.m.
	10/4/18		Field Companies ordered to make a reconnaissance of CHATEAU de la HAIE	
			Switch preparatory to commencing work on same. Baths in Reserve area	p.m.
			improved and water supply for horses maintained and improved.	
	11/4/18		Divisional Commander addressed 428 and 429 Field Companies assembled at	
			PAS with the 126 Infy. Bde. at 2.30 p.m. and 427 Fd. Coy. together with 1/7 Batt.	
			North'd Fusiliers Pioneers at AUTHIE at 3.15 p.m. Orders issued to Fd. Coys. at

Army Form C. 2118.

WAR DIARY
or
INTELLIGENCE SUMMARY.
(Erase heading not required.)

Instructions regarding War Diaries and Intelligence Summaries are contained in F. S. Regs., Part II. and the Staff Manual respectively. Title pages will be prepared in manuscript.

Place	Date	Hour	Summary of Events and Information	Remarks and references to Appendices
		11.30 p.m.	to move on 12th inst to COIGNEUX Valley, J.Mc., to look on LA HAIE Switch, transport and 1 Section remaining behind.	MW
	12/4/18		Field Coy., less transport & 1 Section and Pionier Batt" moved to wood J.17.c., work completed by 12 noon, and commenced work on the Chateau de la HAIE Switch. Transport lines of 427 Field Coy and 1 Section moved from VAUCHELLES to WARNIMONT WOOD, I.23.6.5.8.	MW
	13/4/18		Work continued on Chateau de la HAIE Switch. Warning order issued to Field Coys and Pionier Batt" regarding action to be taken in case of proposed German attack.	MW
	14/4/18		428 Fd Coy Transport lines move to HENU. HqQrs R.E. moved from billets into bivouac accommodation in Chateau grounds, PAS. Orders received in afternoon for Division to relieve 37th Division on nights 16/17th, 17th/18th April. Orders for relief of Christmas R.E. and Pionier Battalions issued late at night.	MW
	15/4/18		428 Fd Coy relieved 154 Fd Coy R.E. 1 Section remaining on Transport Lines, which also relieved 154 Fd Coy transport lines. Location of Coy Hdqrs E.28.a.1.7., transport lines J.3.6.6.	
	16/4/18		HqQrs R.E. relieved HqQrs R.E. 37 Division and moved to COIN, J.10.s.s. 429 Fd Cy Coy relieved 153 Fd Coy R.E. and moved to E.23.c.3.0. transport to J.9.a.4.2. The mounted section with officers were attached to Hqrs R.E. for work under orders of	MW

WAR DIARY / INTELLIGENCE SUMMARY

(Erase heading not required.)

Place	Date	Hour	Summary of Events and Information	Remarks and references to Appendices
COURT	17/4/18 – 22/4/18		Geo. Section. B.G.R.A. 42nd Division. 429 Fd. Coy. Matured 152 Field Coy RE and moved to J18.b.30. Transport and 1 Section to J3.b.56.	MW
			Field Companies and Companies of Pioneers put under orders of Infy. Bdes. for work. Water and Roads Officers employed on investigating, reinforcing water supply and roads. Check work of Field Coys and Construction of Strong points in Purple System, maintenance and improvement of trenches.	MW
	23/4/18		429 Fd Cy RE and the two Companies of Pioneers working with right and right-centre Brigades withdrawn for urgent work of accommodating a Battalion in wood from SAILLY au BOIS to Chateau de la HAIE. Infantry and transport divided to create necessary shelters to be drawn from near dumps.	MW
	24/4/18		Work on section of shelters commenced. 429 Fd Cy RE Wagons withdrawn to transport lines, coming under orders of CRE. Three sections remained in old billets at SAILLY, but certain men from each Section withdrawn to form a Coy site Section in transport lines for providing accommodation there. The reserve section	MW
	25/4/18		of 423 Field Coy rejoined its Company in forward billets. Section of 427 Fd Cy (less "Russ" (Muzzoor) rejoined its Company and upland by a Section	

Army Form C. 2118.

WAR DIARY
or
INTELLIGENCE SUMMARY.
(Erase heading not required.)

Instructions regarding War Diaries and Intelligence Summaries are contained in F. S. Regs., Part II. and the Staff Manual respectively. Title pages will be prepared in manuscript.

Place	Date	Hour	Summary of Events and Information	Remarks and references to Appendices
			Of the 409 R Riddick Coy RE One Company of Pioneers placed at disposal of 126th Inf. Bde, One Company renamed at disposal of 125 Inf. Bde and third Company working with 409 Fd Coy under CRE's orders.	
	26/4/18		Work commenced by 409 R Co., & one Co. of Pioneers on string points on Purple Line in sight of Divisional Scales.	APP B
	27/4/18		Work continues.	
	28/4/18		Heads rarr Iwi Roads greatly improved. Stables at CHATEAU DE LA HAIE completed. Section 409 FA Coy supped back temporarily to Transport Lines. Major J G RIDDICK 409 field Co proceeds to 156 Infantry Bgd. for attachment. Capt J ENTWISTLE took over temporary command of the Company.	APP B
	29/4/18		Transport Lines of 428 and 409 Field Companies had to be moved nearer OIGNEUX on account of Village being Rifle range. Capt A N WALKER Adjutant RE 2nd in command temporarily. Lieut N H BATEMAN being up to duties of Adjutant temporarily. WALKER Orders received for Lieut Col A N LAWFORD to resume Coy HQ bringing to join 155 Corps as CRE 155 Corps troops on 1st May 1918.	(std)
	30/4/18		409 Field C RE continued to work on HIGH STREET. Other Companies continued work on above, viz: Digging & wiring strong points and reserve trenches, clearing old German trenches, gas proofing, maintaining roads & water supply, and work for RA.	APP B

War Diary
Vol. 16.

Confidential

H.Q. R.E. 42nd Division

May, 1918

Volume A.

H.Q. R.E. 42nd Division

Reference Map 57DNE 1/20,000

WAR DIARY
or
INTELLIGENCE SUMMARY.
(Erase heading not required.)

Army Form C. 2118.

Instructions regarding War Diaries and Intelligence Summaries are contained in F.S. Regs., Part II. and the Staff Manual respectively. Title pages will be prepared in manuscript.

Place	Date	Hour	Summary of Events and Information	Remarks and references to Appendices
COUIN	1/5/18	—	42nd Divl. R.E. concentrated on Defence work in Central Sector IV Corps Front. Lieut. Col. N.V. Rowbotham proceeded to take over duties as C.R.E. XV Corps Group. Captain C.F.T. Jones took over temporary command of 42/29 Field Co. R.E.	COUIN
	2/4/18	—	Major J.G. RIDDICK commanding 428 Field Co. R.E. vice Lt. Col. A.V. LAWFORD. A/2nd Lieut Field Co. R.E. Captain J. ENTWISTLE, 428 Field Co. R.E. appointed to command 427 Field Co. R.E. Captain (Temp) A.V. WALKER (Adjutant Hd 3 Divnl. R.E. appointed second in command 428 Field Co. R.E.	COUIN
	3/5/18	—	Lieut. W.H. BATEMAN, appointed Adjutant H.Q. Divl. R.E. vacancy filled in 6th Inf. by 57th Divl. R.E.	COUIN
	11/5/18	—	Orders issued re field relief of 62nd Divl. R.E. by 57th Divl. R.E. on C.R.E. and.	COUIN
	6/5/18	—	Work carried on Defences. Field. Coy. Commdrs. of relieving Divisions show round works.	COUIN
	8/5/18	—	437 Field Co. R.E. were relieved by 505 Field Co. R.E. and moved into Rest Billets at HENU. 428 Field Co. R.E. were relieved by 421 Field Co. R.E., and moved to Bois de ST PIERRE, near PAS. 429 Field Co. R.E. were relieved by 502 N Field Co R.E. and moved to COUIN.	COUIN

WAR DIARY
or
INTELLIGENCE SUMMARY.
(Erase heading not required.)

Army Form C. 2118.

Place	Date	Hour	Summary of Events and Information	Remarks and references to Appendices
GOIN P.A.S.	6/5/18	—	C.R.E. Indian Division handed over to C.R.E. 57th Division and moved into rest area at P.A.S.	contd
	7/5/18	—	Field Coys. engaged moving in cleaning up Equipment and Transport. Orders for Army Orders were issued to all ranks to be prepared to move at short notice by night and by lorries motor lorry by day. Suitable form of wg of tools and Dumps kept in S.Os. were carried with Field Cos.	contd
	8/5/18		419 Indian C.R.E. Engineers worked on Engineering work. 418 (Kent) Field Co engaged [illeg] over [illeg] a yards and filling in R.O. 0 - 10 May. 420 Field Co R.E. Engaged on Rifle Ranges for 170 Inf Bde & 171 Bde also Mess and occupied M Tanks continuing.	contd
	9/5/18		419 Indian C.R.E. Continued work on Tunnels & Dugouts & went to right Brigade. 418 Kent Field [illeg] [illeg] [illeg] continued [illeg] [illeg] [illeg] work 420 Field Co R.E. Continued Training Programme but there was no [illeg] 419 Inf Bde 419 Field Co Complete work on Box YAPKE (LAIDDIE) and BAYENCOURT SWITCHES, preparing from Rifle Rangs of Right Support [illeg] developments & Drill, and Box BAYENCOURT to BAYENCOURT SWITCH in reference to work.	contd
	12/5/18		PURPLE SWITCH 419 Field Co R.E. continued work on work.	contd
	13/5/18		420 Tunnelling Coy not employed. Men not employed on work [illeg] training Programme.	contd

Sheet III

WAR DIARY
or
INTELLIGENCE SUMMARY
(Erase heading not required.)

Army Form C.2118.

Place	Date	Hour	Summary of Events and Information	Remarks and references to Appendices
P.A.S.	19/9/18		428 Field Co. carried out Rifle Practice on Rifle Range. Other Coys. carried out works as shown. Brown Sector of 307th Infantry Regiment, U.S.A. Army attached to 427 Field Co. R.E. for training.	Cont'd
	24/9/18		Works continued. 428 Field Co. engaged on erection of Huts for American Army Battalions recently arrived.	Cont'd
	24/25/9/18		Work on construction of Check Dug-outs continued by 427 Field Co. who were assisted by section of 428 Field Co.	Cont'd
	25/9/18		429 Field Co. engaged on Dug-outs and Strong Points on Ruyaulcourt Switch. Erection of Dumps commenced at PAS and HENU by 428's Field Co. On the 19th CRE held a Conference of Field Coy Commanders and O.C. 4th North Iris (R.) & C. Pioneer Battn. 307th a Inf. Bde. U.S. Army. Major J.O.L. Riddell left HQ 126th Inf. Bde. (where he had been temporarily attached for duty) and came to HQ R.E. for temporary duty.	Cont'd
	26/9/18		Works continued on Dug-outs and Strong Points. Training Programme continued by units of Troops. Divisional Commander inspected Trench Riding & Entrenching other works of 427 & 428 Field Coys. A section of each Coy took part in ceremonial parade.	Cont'd

Army Form C. 2118.

WAR DIARY
or
INTELLIGENCE SUMMARY.
(Erase heading not required.)

Abt IV

Place	Date	Hour	Summary of Events and Information	Remarks and references to Appendices
PAS	27/9/18 to 30/9/18		Work on Newel Dugouts and Defences continued on Lining Mines as about VB. Digging and wiring Strong Point at CHATEAU DE LA HAIE and Battalion H.Q. of the Left and Reserve Brigades.	APB
	30/9/18		Divisional Commander presented medal ribbons to 1 Officer and 6 or. of 429 Field Co R.E. Major J.G. Roderick left HQ R.E. to take over command of 429 Field Co R.E.	APB

W P Bateman
Col. R.E. (T).
Adjt. for C.R.E.
42ND (E. LANCS) DIV.

Army Form C. 2118.

WAR DIARY
or
INTELLIGENCE SUMMARY.
(Erase heading not required.)

Vol 17

War Diary
of
H.Q. R.E. 42nd Division
from 1st June, 1918 to 30th June, 1918

VOLUME IV

H.Q. R.E.
42nd Division

Army Form C. 2118.

Reference Map 57D. 1/40,000

WAR DIARY
or
INTELLIGENCE SUMMARY.
(Erase heading not required.)

Place	Date	Hour	Summary of Events and Information	Remarks and references to Appendices
PAS.	1/6/18	—	Orders received for relief of 57th Division by 42nd Division, and CRE's orders issued accordingly. Move cancelled later. Advance parties of 3 Field Coys. who had proceeded to Field Coys. of that Division recalled. 427 Field Co. R.E. engaged on dugouts at HENU, 428 Field Co. R.E. on hutting at Rest Camp, HALLOY, and 429 Field Co. R.E. continued work on tunnelled dugouts in BAYENCOURT and LE HAIE (Pamph.) Dovetales.	CRE
	2/6/18			CRE
	3/6/18		Orders received for relief of N.Z. Division by 42nd Division. Orders accordingly issued by CRE to 3 Field Coys. for relief of N.Z. Divisional RE in HEBUTERNE (Right) Sector II Corps. front. Advance parties from each Field Coy. proceeded to be attached to Field Coys. of N.Z. Engineers, and take over work in progress.	CRE
	4/6/18		Works as above continued.	CRE
	5/6/18	—	428 Field Co. R.E. completed hutting at 42nd Divnl. Rest Camp, HALLOY. 427 and 429 Field Coys. engaged on works. H.Q. R.E. sent representative to take over N.Z. Divisional R.E. Dump at BERTRANCOURT.	CRE
	6/6/18		427 Field Coy. continued work on tunnelled Dugouts. 428 and 429 Field Coys. completed works, and spent half day cleaning harness, vehicles, etc.	CRE
	7/6/18		427th Field Co. moved to billets near BERTRANCOURT, J.33.a.2.2 taking over from 3rd Field Co. N.Z.E. Works taken over consisted of tunnelled dugouts and repairs to trenches.	CRE

WAR DIARY
or
INTELLIGENCE SUMMARY.
(Erase heading not required.)

Army Form C. 2118.

Place	Date	Hour	Summary of Events and Information	Remarks and references to Appendices
PAS.	7/6/18		428 Field Co. moved to Bus Woods being in reserve. 429 Field Co. moved to SAINSY-AU-BOIS. J.19 c.42. taking over from 1st Field Co. N.Z.E. Transport of 3 Field Coys moved to camp on BUS-LOUVENCOURT Road, J.31.6. H.Q. R.E. moved to BUS. taking over from C.R.E. N.Z. Division. Thro' completed American Pioneers attached to 429 Field Co. rejoined 307th American Infantry Regiment. 427 Field Co. engaged on mined and tunnelled dugouts at J.34 c.6.8. (½ A.F. 57th N.E. and (5½ D.S.E.) and general defence work, under direction of Infantry Bde., in Right Sub. Sect. 428 Field Co. made reconnaissance of Catacombs in BUS Chateau galleries at a lower depth. The present workings are reached by two vertical shafts, which were originally air shafts. Also on mined dug out and surface Observation Post at FORT BERTHA. 1 Section of 428 Field Co. detached on permanent R.A. R.E. work whilst Company is in reserve. 429 Field Co. on defence works.	OMB OMB
BUS-LES-ARTOIS.	8/6/18			
	9/6/18		C.R.E. held conference at H.Q. R.E. of Field Coy. Commanders, and outlined programme of work to be undertaken whilst Divisions are in the Line. Works continued by Field Coys. as above.	OMB

Army Form C. 2118.

WAR DIARY
or
INTELLIGENCE SUMMARY.
(Erase heading not required.)

Instructions regarding War Diaries and Intelligence Summaries are contained in F. S. Regs. Part II. and the Staff Manual respectively. Title pages will be prepared in manuscript.

Place	Date	Hour	Summary of Events and Information	Remarks and references to Appendices
BUS-LES-ARTOIS	10.6.18		427 Field Co. engaged mainly on Defence Works and Artillery Brigade H.Q. at J.33.c.10. 428 Field Co. engaged on D.H.Q. dugout at I.23 central, and winding rooms at LOUVENCOURT Station for stretcher and walking wounded. 429 Field Co. engaged on defence works at FORT HEROD, FORT HOD and FORT STEWART. Works according to programme continued, 429 Field Co. digging out winning three forts referred to above.	contd
	11/6/18		As above.	contd
	12/6/18		428 Field Co. engaged on Huts in BUS in Bois Road at 42.U.S. Batt M.G.C. 427 and 429 Field Coys on Tunnellers Dugouts and Forts.	contd
	13/6/18		429 Field Co. were engaged mainly on Bed and Cover dugouts at 127 c.63.95 and K.19.c.8.2. also repairing, deepening, and widening trenches at Railway Avenue, Canterbury Avenue, Hope Sentl and Railway Avenue. 428 Field Co. reconnoitred site for Corduroy Road for A.R.P. at I.24.d. 429 Field Co. engaged on wiring Forts HEROD HOD and STEWART.	contd
	15/6/18		Field Coys. continued works, but owing to Inf. Brigade relief no working parties were found by 125 and 127 Brigades.	contd
	16/6/18		428 Field Co. took over two R.A. dugouts from 429 Field Co. at J.24.c.8.9. and J.24.c.4.5. 429 Field Co. engaged on dugouts, tracks, and gas-proofing dugouts. Gas blankets were fixed at Coy H.Q. Q.2.d.5.9. and T.M. B. H.Q. at K.32.a.2.6.	contd

A.5834. Wt. W.4973/M687. 750,000 8/16 D. D. & L. Ltd. Forms/C.2118/13.

WAR DIARY
or
INTELLIGENCE SUMMARY.
(Erase heading not required.)

Army Form C. 2118.

Place	Date	Hour	Summary of Events and Information	Remarks and references to Appendices
BUS LES ARTOIS.	17/6/18 to 19/6/18		427 Field Co. engaged on tunnel and trailer dug out, and repairs were effected to Cut and Cover dug out at X.32.a.7.7. 428 Field Co. engaged on works as per programme. Hutting at LOUVENCOURT Station completed. 429 Field Co. commenced deep dug out at FORT HEROD, X.13.6.6.9.	Contd
	20/6/18		Works as per above carried out. 427 Field Co. duck boarding trenches and building fire Bays.	Contd
	21/6/18		6. R.E. H.2. & Division proceeded to England on 14 days' leave. Major J.H. MOUSLEY D.S.O. O.C. 427 Field Co. took over duties as Y.C.R.E.	Contd
	22/6/18 to 30/6/18		The 3 Field Co.ys continued programme of works. 427 Field Co. erected splinter proof shelters for ammunition dumps in Railway Cuttings, and furnishing Brigade, Battalion, and Company HQ. Three 428 Field Co. completed Corduroy Road at ARP (12n.d.). This road is 300 yards long and 12 ft. wide. Two gas proof cut and cover dug outs were commenced for reception of stretcher cases from main Dressing Station in case of gas attack. 429 Field Co. took on works at FORT HOD, Horse and Engine shed in progress for lighting set in SAILLY Catacombs. Additions to existing accommodation at dug out (X.17.c.31) was put in hand. On the 28th Major J.H. MOUSLEY, D.S.O. Y.C.R.E. proceeded to ÉTAPLES on 5 days sick leave, Major J.G. RIDDICK 429 Field Co. taking over duties as Y.C.R.E.	Contd

WAR DIARY
or
INTELLIGENCE SUMMARY.

(Erase heading not required.)

Army Form C. 2118.

Place	Date	Hour	Summary of Events and Information	Remarks and references to Appendices
BUS-LES-ARTOIS.			2nd Field Co. N.Z. Engineers were working under orders of C.R.E. 42nd Div. from 7th inst. to 30th. In forward area on erection of wire, tunnelled, and cut and cover dugouts, also repair of trenches and wiring of forts and strong points. During the month 2 Sections of 179 and 1 section of 252 Tunnelling Coys R.E. were working under orders of C.R.E. 42nd Division and were engaged on Tunnelled and Timber dugouts for Brigade, Battalion, and Coy. Head Qrs. Roads in Divisional Area were constantly patrolled and kept in order under supervision of Officer attached from 1/9th Battalion North Fus. (P) who had permanent working parties from Divisional Battle Surplus. Water arrangements were also kept in good order and repair by Divisional R.E. under supervision of an Officer attached from 1/9th Batt. North Fus. (P)	BWB BWB

Bateman
Captain R.E.
Adjt. for C.R.E. 42nd Division

SECRET.

Copy No..16..

C.R.E., 42nd (East Lancs.) Division Order No. 39.
- by -
LIEUT.COLONEL R.E.B. PRATT, D.S.O., R.E.

Ref. Maps :- 57 D.N.E. 1/20,000
57 D.S.E. 1/20,000
57 D.   1/40,000

Monday, 3rd June, 1918.

---

1. 42nd Division (less Artillery) is relieving the N.Z. Division (less Artillery) in the right sector IV Corps Front, on the nights 6th/7th and 7th/8th June.

2. Infantry reliefs are to be carried out as follows :-
   Night 6th/7th June. 127th Inf. Bde. will relieve 1st N.Z. Inf. Bde. in the left sub-sector.
   Night 7th/8th June. 126th Inf. Bde. will relieve the 2nd N.Z. Inf. Bde. in the right subsector.
   7th June. 125 Inf. Bde. will relieve 3rd New Zealand (Rifle) Bde. in Divisional Reserve.

3. Between 6th and 8th June 42nd Division is being relieved in Left Reserve Divisional Area by 37th Division.

4. Moves and reliefs of Field Companies R.E. and Pioneer Battalions will take place in accordance with attached table.

5. (a) Os.C. concerned will arrange details direct and will take over from opposite numbers in N.Z. Division all defence schemes, programmes of work, work in hand, documents, plans and trench maps, etc. relating to same together with all bridging and demolition schemes.
   (b) Copies of lists of all area stores and the numbers of all secret maps taken over will be submitted to this Office by 6 p.m. 9th instant.
   (c) All defence schemes, programmes of work, work in hand, documents, plans, trench maps, etc. now in possession of 42nd Divisional R.E. and Pioneers will be handed over to corresponding units of 37th Division.

6. Command of the right sector and of the Artillery covering that sector will pass to G.O.C. 42nd Division at 12 midnight 7th/8th June.

7. R.E. party now with 42nd Divisional Artillery will receive orders later.

8. (a) R.S.M. SORRAY, R.E. with the usual permanent staff and an infantry party of 2 N.C.Os. and 20 O.R. will take over at the R.E. Dump, BERTRANCOURT by 12 noon 6th instant, arriving at the dump two hours earlier to arrange details.
   (b) N.Z. Field Company dumps will be taken over by relieving field companies of 42nd Division.
   (c) C.R.E. 42nd Division will continue to staff the R.E. Dumps at PAS and HENU until the relieving party from 37th Division arrives at 12 noon on 7th instant.

9. (a) Field Companies R.E. 42 Divn. will move by sections at 200 yards intervals.
   (b) Relief of Field Companies R.E. and Pioneer Battalions will be completed by 12 noon on the 7th instant.
   (c) Completion of moves and reliefs will be reported by wiring the Code word FIN.

10. Communication between C.R.E. and Field Companies 42nd Division will be as laid down in No. R.E. 30 paras. 1A (a) and (b), 2 (a),(b) and (c).

11. Headquarters R.E. will close at PAS at 4 p.m. 7th instant and will re-open at same hour at D.H.Q., BUS-les-ARTOIS.

12. Instructions regarding the Pioneer Section 307th Regiment, U.S. Army now working with 427th Field Coy. R.E. are being issued by 42nd Division.

(Over)

13. C.R.Es. N.Z. and 37th Divisions, Field Companies R.E. and Pioneer Battalion 42nd Division, PLEASE ACKNOWLEDGE.

[signature]
Capt. & Adjt.,
42nd Divisional R.E.

Issued by D.R.L.S. by 11.20 p.m. 3/6/1918.
ORDERLY

Distribution :-

Copy No. 1. 'G', 42nd Division.
2. 'A' and 'Q' 42nd Division.
3. 427 Field Coy. R.E.
4. 428 Field Coy. R.E.
5. 429 Field Coy. R.E.
6. 1/7th North'd. Fus. (P).
7. C.R.E. N.Z. Division.
8. C.R.E. 37th Division.
9. C.R.A., 42nd Division.
10. 125th Inf. Bde.
11. 126th Inf. Bde.
12. 127th Inf. Bde.
13. C.E. IV Corps.
14. 42nd Divnl. Train.
15. Lt. Statler, O.C. Pioneer Section, 307th Inf. Regt., U.S. ARMY.
16. War Diary.
17. File.
18. Spare.

Table of Moves and Reliefs to Accompany C.R.E.- 42nd Division, Order No. 39, dated 3rd June, 1918.

Serial No.	Date.	Unit of 42nd Division.	From	TO Unit H.Q.	Sector.	Relieves (Unit of N.Z. Divn.)	Relieved by (Unit of 37th Divn.)	Remarks.
1.	7th June.	429 Fld. Coy. R.E.	COUIN.	W. of SAILLY J.17.c.1.2.	Left sub-sector.	1st Fld. Coy. N.Z. Eng.	152 Fld. Coy. R.E.	Reliefs to be completed by 12 noon 7th June.
2.	do.	428 Fld. Coy. R.E.	PAS.	N. of BUS J.20.b.5.0.	Divisional Reserve.	2nd Fld. Coy. N.Z. Eng.	153 Fld. Coy. R.E.	
3.	do.	427 Fld. Coy. R.E.	HENU.	BEMETRANCOURT J.33.a.2.1.	Right sub-sector.	3rd Fld. Coy. N.Z. Eng.	154 Fld. Coy. R.E.	
4.	do.	1/7th North'd. Fus. (P).	COIGNEUX.	S. of BUS J.32.cent.		N.Z. Maori (P) Battn.	1/9th North Staffs. (P).	

Note :- 2nd Field Coy. N.Z.E. is remaining (together with 1st N.Z. Inf. Bde. and one M.G. Coy. N.Z. Divn.) as reserve to 42nd Division. This Coy. (2nd Fld. Coy. N.Z.E.) is standing fast in its present location at J.20.c.3.9. O.C. 428 Field Coy. R.E., though taking over work from this Company will therefore take over the camp of the 154th Field Coy. R.E. at J.20.b.5.0.

SECRET.   Copy No. 6

Amendment No. 1 to C.R.E. 42nd Division Order No. 39.

Tuesday, 4th June, 1918.

As a result of the move of the 37th Division out of the IV Corps Area, the following corrections will be made to above order :-

1. Para. 3.   For "37th Division" read "N.Z. Division."

2. Para. 5 (c) For "37th Division" read "N.X. Division."

3. Para. 8 is cancelled and the following substituted :-

   (a) An advance party will be sent to take over the R.E. Dump BERTRANCOURT at 10 a.m. 6th instant. C.R.E. N.Z. Division is sending a similar party to PAS Dump. Dumps will be finally relieved by 12 noon on 7th instant. *At Same Loca*

   (b) New Zealand Field Company Dumps will be taken over by relieving Field Companies of 42nd Division.

   (c) HENU R.E. Dump is being taken over by 3rd Field Coy. N.Z.E.

4. **Table of moves and reliefs.**

   The whole column "Relieved by" will be amended to read as follows :-

        Serial No. 1.   1st Field Coy. N.Z.E.
        Serial No. 2.   "   "   "   "
        Serial No. 3   3rd Field Coy. N.Z.E.
        Serial No. 4   N.Z. Maori (P) Battn.

                                        W. Bateman
                                        Capt. & Adjt.,
                                        42nd Divisional R.E.

Issued by D.R.L.S. at   p.m. 4/6/1918.

DISTRIBUTION :-   Copy No. 1.   427 Field Coy. R.E.
                            2.   428 Field Coy. R.E.
                            3.   429 Field Coy. R.E.
                            4.   1/7th North'd. Fus. (P).
                            5.   C.R.E., N.Z. Division.
                            6.   War Diary.
                            7.   Spare.File.
                            8.   Spare.

SECRET.   Copy No. 14

C.R.E., 42nd (East Lancs.) Division, Order No. 37.
- by -
LIEUT. COLONEL R.E.B. PRATT, D.S.O., R.E.

Ref. Map.- 1/20,000 57D. N.E.   Saturday, 1st June, 1918.
----

1.   The 42nd Division (less Artillery) is relieving the 57th Division (less artillery) in the Centre Sector IV Corps Front on the nights 4th/5th and 5th/6th June.

2.   Infantry reliefs are to be carried out as follows :-
   Night 4th/5th June.   126th Inf. Bde. will relieve 172 Inf. Bde. in the left sub-sector.
   Night 5th/6th June   127 Inf. Bde. will relieve 171 Inf. Bde. in the right sub-sector.
   5th June.   125th Inf. Bde. will relieve 170 Inf. Bde. in Divisional Reserve.

3. (a) Field Companies R.E. and Pioneer Battalion of 42nd Division will relieve similar units of 57th Division as follows :-

42 Div. Unit.	57 Div. Unit.	Headquarters.	Horse Lines.	Remarks.
427 Fld. Coy relieves	505 Field Coy.	E.28.c.98.70	J.9.a.4.2.	Right Sector.
429 Fld. Coy. relieves	421 Field Coy.	E.28.d.70.65	J.3.b.1.5.	Left Sector.
428 Fld. Coy. relieves	502 Field Coy.	J.3.b.3.4.	J.3.b.3.4.	Divl. Reserve.
Pioneer Battn. relieves	Pioneer Battn.	J.3.c.40.15	J.3.c.15.15	One Coy. H.Q. - E.28.c.9.7. One Coy. H.Q. - E.28.d.80.75. One Company - 2 platoons - K.4.a.60.45. 2 platoons, -

   (b) The 428th Field Coy. R.E. and the respective transport of 42nd Divisional R.E. and Pioneer Battalion will relieve by 4 p.m. on the 5th instant.
        The remainder of the relief will be carried out on the night 5th/6th June, and will be completed by 2 a.m. 6th June.

   (c) Field Companies R.E. of 57th Division will relieve Field Companies R.E. of 42nd Division as follows :-
        421st Field Coy. R.E. will relieve 427th Field Coy. R.E.
        502nd Field Coy. R.E. will relieve 429th Field Coy. R.E.
        505th Field Coy. R.E. will relieve 428th Field Coy. R.E.

4.   Os.C. concerned will arrange details direct and will take over all defence schemes, programmes of work and work in hand, documents, plans and trench maps, etc. relating to same, together with all bridging and demolition schemes.
     Lists of all area stores and numbers of all Secret Maps taken over will be submitted to this office by 6 p.m. 7th instant.

5.   All defence schemes, programmes of work, work in hand, documents, plans, trench maps, etc. now in possession of 42nd Divisional R.E. and Pioneers will be handed over to corresponding units of 57th Division.

6.   Command of the Artillery covering the Centre Sector of IV Corps Front will pass to B.G.R.A. 42nd Division at 6 p.m. 5th June.
     The party of eight sappers from 428th Field Coy. R.E. under

2/Lieut. Chapman, R.E. will continue to work under the Orders of the B.G.R.A. 42nd Division.

7. (a) O.C. 1/7th North'd. Fus. (Pnrs.) will appoint one officer to act as Roads Officer, and one officer as Trench Tramway Officer. The officers so appointed will arrange to meet corresponding officers of the 57th Division, not later than 3rd instant to take over the work.

   (b) The Water Supply Officer 42nd Division will take over the duties from Water Supply Officer, 57th Division.

8. RS.M. SOWRAY, R.E. with the usual permanent staff and an infantry party of two N.C.Os. and 20 O.R. will take over at the R.E. Dump, SOUASTRE by 4 p.m. 5th instant.

9. Field Company dumps will be taken over by relieving Field Companies.

10. The usual intervals will be observed on the march.

11. Communication between C.R.E. and Field Companies will be as laid down in R.E. 30 paras. 1A(a) and (b) and 2(a), (b) and (c).

12. Completion of moves and reliefs will be be reported by wiring the Code Word FIN.

13. Command of the Centre Sector IV Corps Front will pass to G.O.C. 42nd Division at 12 midnight 5th/6th June.

14. H.Q.R.E. will close at PAS at 4 p.m. on 5th June and will re-open at same hour at D.H.Q. COUIN.

15. Orders regarding the attached pioneers from the 307th Inf. Regt. U.S. Army will be issued later.

16. C.R.E. 57th Division, 42nd Divisional R.E. and Pioneer Battalion PLEASE ACKNOWLEDGE.

                                    Capt. & Adjt.,
                                    for C.R.E., 42nd Division.

Issued by D.R.L.S. at 12.50 p.m. 1/6/1918.
          ORDERLY

DISTRIBUTION :-
       Copy No. 1. 42nd Divn. 'G'.
               2. 42nd Divn. 'A' and 'Q'.
               3. 427 Field Coy. R.E.
               4. 428 Field Coy. R.E.
               5. 429 Field Coy. R.E.
               6. O.C. 1/7th North'd. Fus. (Pnrs.)
               7. C.R.E. 57th Division.
               8. C.R.A., 42nd Division.
               9. 125 Inf. Bde.
              10. 126 Inf. Bde.
              11. 127 Inf. Bde.
              12. C.E. IV Corps.
              13. O.C. 42nd Divnl. Train.
              14. War Diary.
              15. File.
              16. Lt. Statler, O.C. Pnr. Section, 307th Inf. Regt.
                        U.S. Army.
              17. Spare.
              18. Spare.

SECRET.   Copy No. 6
                           (WARNING)
         C.R.E., 42nd (East Lancs.) Division,/Order No. 38.
                              - by -
              LIEUT. COLONEL F.E.B. PIATT, D.S.O., R.E.

Ref:- Map.
                                                Saturday, 1st June, 1918.

1.   C.R.E. 42nd Division Order No. 37 dated 1/6/1918 is cancelled.

2.   The 42nd Division (less Artillery) is relieving the N.Z. Division
(less Artillery) in Right Sector, IV Corps Front.

3.   The following reliefs and moves will probably take place :-
     (a) Night 6th/7th June.
         The 127th Inf. Brigade and 1 Battn. 125th Inf. Brigade will
             relieve the 1st N.Z. Inf. Brigade.
         Brigade H.Qrs. Catacombs, SAILLY-au-BOIS.

     (b) Night 7th/8th June.
         The 126th Inf. Brigade and 1 Battn. 125th Inf. Brigade will
             proceed by bus from PAS to BERTRANCOURT and will relieve
             the 2nd N.Z. Inf. Brigade.
         Brigade H.Qrs. J.24.d.6.9.

     (c) 7th June.
         125th Inf. Brigade & H.Qrs. move to ST. LEGER-les-AUTHIES.
         1 Battn. 125th Inf. Brigade moves to ROSSIGNOL FARM.

N.B. Battalions of 125th Inf. Brigade attached to 126th and 127th
Inf. Brigade will be used as Brigade Reserve Battns.

4.   The 37th Division will side step into present 42nd Divisional
area as units of 42nd Division move away to relieve the N.Z. Division.
N.Z. Division Units on relief by 42nd Division will move into present
37th Divisional Area.

5.   The 307th Regt. U.S.A. Army will be concentrated in 126th Inf.
Brigade Camp at PAS. Detailed orders will be issued later.

7.   ACKNOWLEDGE.

                                                    [signature]
                                                    Capt. & Adjt.,
                                                    42nd Divisional R.E.
Issued by D.R.L.S. at   p.m. 1/6/1918.
          ORDERLY

Distribution :-

     Copy No. 1.   427 Field Coy. R.E.
          2.   428 Field Coy. R.E.
          3.   429 Field Coy. R.E.
          4.   1/7th North'd. Fus. (Pnrs.)
          5.   File.
          6.   War Diary.
          7.   Spare.

Confidential
ORIGINAL

Vol 18

WAR DIARY

H.Q. R.E. 42nd DIVISION

Volume 4.

ORIGINAL

Headquarters 42nd Divisional RE

Army Form C. 2118.

WAR DIARY
or
INTELLIGENCE SUMMARY.
(Erase heading not required.)

Instructions regarding War Diaries and Intelligence Summaries are contained in F. S. Regs., Part II. and the Staff Manual respectively. Title pages will be prepared in manuscript.

Reference Map 57 D 1/40000

Place	Date	Hour	Summary of Events and Information	Remarks and references to Appendices
BUS-les-ARTOIS	1/7/18		Division holding Right Sector IV Corps Front, with 2 Brigade in line and 1 in Reserve. 429 Field Coy RE with Right Brigade, 428 Field Co RE with Left Brigade, and 428 Field Co RE with Brigade in Reserve. Hd. Qrs RE at BUS. Major J. G. RIDDICK (O.C. 429 Field CoRE) acting C.R.E. 429 Field Coy employed on improvement of Communication trenches and in the construction of dug-outs. 429 Field Coy working on Defended Localities, tunnelled dug-outs, shelters, huts and electric lighting of SAILLY Catacombs. 428 on general defensive work, including localities, M.G. positions and improvements to trenches tunnelled dug-outs, wiring and miscellaneous jobs	(sgd)
	2/7/18 to 19.7.15		428 Field Coy on same work generally as on 1st. New work being undertaken as other jobs comp (etc)	(sgd)
	2.7.18		Bertain of 429 Field Coys jobs taken over by N.Z.s owing alteration of Northern boundary of Divisional Sector	(sgd)
			4 Sappers killed, & 2 sappers wounded, all of 429 FIELD CoRE, by shell fire on 2nd inst.	
	3/7/18 to 22/7/15		429 Field Coy employed on tunnelled dug-outs, localities, wiring and dug-outs for M.G. positions.	(sgd)
	8.7.18		Capt. (Actg Major) A.T. Shakespear, D.S.O., M.C. RE (Staff Officer to CE 5yth Army) appointed CRE 42nd Division with acting rank of Lt. Col.	(sgd)
	12.7.18		Lt. Col Shakespear appointed CRE 12th Div.	(sgd)
	12.7.18		Major J.G. Riddick, O.C. 429 Field CoRE, appointed CRE 42nd Division, with acting rank of Lt. Colonel, & assumes duties on two date.	(sgd)
	8/7/18 to 18/7/18		428 Field CoRE employed on localities and strong points in accordance with new Defense Scheme, etc on dug-outs, trenches and wiring.	(sgd)
AUTHIE.	16.7.18 7.30am		HQRE moved from BUS and established at AUTHIE, with 42nd DHQ	(sgd)
	18/7/18 to 31/7/18		429 Field Coy employed on same work except for slight changes made by new Brigade, and certain strong points which were handed over to 428 Field Coy RE.	(sgd)

WAR DIARY
or
INTELLIGENCE SUMMARY
(Erase heading not required.)

Army Form C. 2118.

Sheet II

Place	Date	Hour	Summary of Events and Information	Remarks and references to Appendices
AUTHIE	23/7/18 to 26.7.18		Main work of 429 Field Coy R.E.: on tunnelled dug-outs.	15mB
	20.7.18		In addition to general works already on hand, 428 Field Coy R.E. completed excavation for and concreting of foundation for Moir Pill Box.	15mB
	21.7.18 to 26.7.18		428 on same general work on localities, trenches, wiring, drainage, roads and dugouts. Moir Pill Box completed on 23rd, on which date not much work was done on localities owing to heavy downpours of rain.	15mB
	25/7/18		Warning Order issued to Field Coys. to be prepared for relief about 30th by Field Coys of 51st Division.	15mB
	27.7.18		Warning Order of 25 inst. cancelled owing to 51st Division being placed in G.H.Q. Reserve.	
	28/7/18 to 31/7/18		Much work had to be done by 427 & 429 Field Coys on revetting and drainage of trenches owing to wet weather. Owing to shortage of working parties for this work sappers and pioneers were taken off certain tunnelled dug-outs which were handed over to Section of 252 Tunnelling Co. The sappers released were put on trench improvements.	15mB
	24/7/18 to 31/7/18		428 Field Coy R.E. on localities, including digging trenches to absolute minimum, drainage, duckboarding, wiring, trustleping, revetting trench shelters. Also erecting Nissen Huts, making reconnaissance of nettles in COLINCAMPS, and much road work and miscellaneous jobs.	15mB
	1/7/18 to 31/7/18		One officer and section of 428 Field Corps R.E., attached to Battery Command Post as technical supervision in construction of dug-outs for R.A. throughout the month giving. Roads in Divisional Area were maintained in a good standard of repair by an attached officer from 412 (North Trio (Pioneers) with an infantry working party from Div. Battle Surplus, the same officer was responsible for patrolling the Water Supply arrangements, executing minor repairs and improvements. A considerable amount of rain fell during the month & made the passage of certain trench (especially C.T.s) & roads difficult at times & rendered an increased amount of work necessary in winter programme is being considered in this connection.	15mB

Capt. R.E.
adj. for CRE 42nd Div.

9R19

WAR DIARY

OF

HD. QRS. 42nd DIVISIONAL R.E.

AUGUST 1918

Vol 4

Confidential
Original

Army Form C. 2118.

WAR DIARY
or
INTELLIGENCE SUMMARY.
(Erase heading not required.)

Instructions regarding War Diaries and Intelligence Summaries are contained in F. S. Regs., Part II. and the Staff Manual respectively. Title pages will be prepared in manuscript.

Place	Date	Hour	Summary of Events and Information	Remarks and references to Appendices
AUTHIE.	1-8-1918 to 14-8-1918		Headqrs. 42nd Divisional RE with 42nd Divisional Headqrs at AUTHIE (SOMME). 429th Field Coy RE working in Right Brigade Sector of the Divisional front on construction of localities with dug-outs for garrison of same, also cut and cover dug-outs for H.Q. G.C. 429 Field Coy RE working in Left Bde Sector, principal work being on tunnelled dug-outs, improvements to trenches and cut and cover shelters. 428 Field Coy RE with Brigade in Reserve engaged on digging of and improvements to trenches, survey &c. Construction of Pill Box at J30 b 7·4. Constructed Road to Advanced DHQ also road to new ADS on J15 b. Construction of Shelters at Strong Points. One Section attached to RA for supervision of works on dug-outs. Additions and improvements to those at COURCELLES and BERTRANCOURT. Various Services for general improvement in Reserve Area and DHQ.	Ah
BUS-LES-ARTOIS	15/8/18		The enemy commenced a retirement on this date. HQ.RE. moved to BUS LES ARTOIS. Consequent upon enemy retirement, the 429th and 429th Field Coys moved forward and were engaged on the making of dry weather tracks, bridging of trenches, and provided Sappers for each Battalion moving forward, for the purpose of searching for "Booby traps". 428 Field Coy. carried on with jobs in hand.	Ah
	25/8/18			Ah
	27/8/18			Ah
	28/8/18		429, 12 and 429th Fld Coys continued on jobs as above. 428 Field Coy proceeded with excavation of a trench for 4" water pipe from Sucrerie (Mailly-Maillet) eastwards	Ah
	29/8/18		428 Fld Coy (with CRE 42 Div) sited storage tank in connection with pumping station at MAILLY Sucrerie	Ah

A Meachern
Lt Col RE

Army Form C. 2118.

WAR DIARY
or
INTELLIGENCE SUMMARY.
(Erase heading not required.)

Instructions regarding War Diaries and Intelligence Summaries are contained in F. S. Regs., Part II. and the Staff Manual respectively. Title pages will be prepared in manuscript.

Place	Date	Hour	Summary of Events and Information	Remarks and references to Appendices
BUS LES ARTUS	23/8/18		428 Field Coy RE moved from BUS WOODS to COURCELLES AU BOIS and at COURCELLES BATHS. 427th and 429 Fid Coys continuing on reconnaissance work and the improvement of tracks.	Ah
	24/8/18		Continued a.a on 23rd.	Ah
EGLINCAMPS	25/8/18		HQ RE moved with HQ 42D Division to EGLINCAMPS. 429th Field Coy working on the PUISIEUX - MIRAUMONT RD and on Water Supply in MIRAUMONT.	Ah
	26/9/18		a.a on 25th.	Ah
Near ACHIET-LE PETIT	27/8/18		HQ RE with 428 DHQ move to L10 b (nr ACHIET LE PETIT) Coys continuing with work a.a on 25th and 26th.	Ah
	28/8/18		429 Fid Co detailed to stand by in readiness to move, with Brigade detailed "for pursuit at one hour's notice.	Ah
	29/8/18		All 3 Coys engaged on Water Supply reconnaissance for Road Mines and "Booby Traps" in MIRAUMONT, IRLES, ACHIET LE PETIT, WARLENCOURT PYS, THILLOY, LIGNY-THILLOY and LE BARQUE.	Ah
GREVILLERS	30/8/18		HQ RE moved to GREVILLERS. Field Coys engaged a.a on 29th. O.C. 429 Fid Co being in touch with Brigade in pursuit for reconnaissance work.	Ah
	31/8/18		Work carried on a.a on 29th and 30th. During the period of enemy retirement, water supply was opened out and developed to meet requirements of troops and horses in the Divisional Area, despite the fact that the enemy had rendered useless a number of existing wells by blowing them in. A great number of road mines and booby traps were sprung and areas which had been considerably damaged were put into a good state of repair.	Ah

W20

War Diary

Headquarters 42nd Divisional R.E.

September 1st to 30th 1918

Vol. 4

War Diary — September 1918

Strength JHQ 42n D we RE   2 Officers 9 OR

bopPatersonn
Capt RE
Adj for CRE 42nDiv

Original

Army Form C. 2118.

WAR DIARY
or
INTELLIGENCE SUMMARY.
(Erase heading not required.)

Sheet 57 c

Instructions regarding War Diaries and Intelligence Summaries are contained in F. S. Regs., Part II. and the Staff Manual respectively. Title pages will be prepared in manuscript.

Month: September

Place	Date	Hour	Summary of Events and Information	Remarks and references to Appendices
GREVILLERS	1st		Hd Qrs 42nd Divl RE (with 42nd DHQ) at GREVILLERS. 429 Field Coy with Bde in line working on reconnaissance of roads and water supply in forward area. 427 Field Coy with Support Bde employed on the development of water supply in THILLOY, LIGNY THILLOY and LE BARQUE. 428 Field Co with Bde in Reserve, engaged on services in the erection of a new DHQ, also on construction of baths at WARLENCOURT EAUCOURT and water supply at PYS.	13AM
	2nd		427 Field Co. engaged as on 1st. 428 Field Co on development of water supply in WARLENCOURT & PYS. 429 Field Co carried on reconnaissance of roads and wells in RIENCOURT and commenced work on the clearing of debris from well at pumping station on the BAPAUME - ALBERT Rd, N. of RIENCOURT.	13AM
	3rd		125th Bde relieves 127 Bde. 429 Still with Bde in line. Owing to enemy retirement Bde moved to VILLERS-AU-FLOS; 429 Field Co moving with Bde, later in the day moving to BARASTRE. 1 Section moving still further forward to BUS and worked on reconnaissance for Booby traps in dug outs. 428 Field Co employed as on 2nd. 2 section of the 427 Field Co moved to VILLERS AU FLOS + erected Horse Watering Points in the village.	13AM
	4th		HQ 42nd Divl RE (with 42nd DHQ) moved to RIENCOURT LES BAPAUME. 429 Field Co with Forward Bde on reconnaissance work. 428 Fld Co moved to VILLERS AU FLOS Wood. Worked on Water Points at RIENCOURT and BARASTRE also provided Sapping for new DHQ. 2 rear sections of 427 joined 2 forward Section at VILLERS AU FLOS.	14AM
	5th		Field Coys continued as on 4th and during the day handed over to Field Corps, N.Z. Division.	5AM
	6th		Division moved into rest. HQ RE (with 42nd DHQ) remained at RIENCOURT, 427 Fd Co moved to THILLOY, 428 Field Co to old Camp between PYS and WARLENCOURT, 429 Fld Co.	6x13
	6/30		The period spent in cleaning up generally and training, also provision of sapper assistance for improvements to camps.	13AM

WAR DIARY or INTELLIGENCE SUMMARY

Army Form C. 2118.

Place	Date	Hour	Summary of Events and Information	Remarks and references to Appendices
IV VELU	21/9/18		HQ RE (with 42 DHQ) moved to I 36 d 81 (SW of VELU). 428 Fd Co (with forward Bde) moved to HAVRINCOURT WOOD. 427 Field Co (with Bde in Support) moved to J 34 a 88 between BERTINCOURT and HERMIES. 429 Field Coy in reserve moved to LE BUCQUIERE.	[sgnd]
	22/9/18		428 worked on repairs to HB of 126 Bde, gas proofing of dug-outs (forward) and gas proofing of water tanks. Continued work on cleaning and deepening TRESCAULT Well. 427" & 429" Field Coys engaged on Water Supply, Baths & various Services in Support reserve area.	[sgnd]
	23rd		428 Field Co continued work on TRESCAULT well and organised parties for reconnoitring and gas-proofing dug-outs across whole Bde front. 427 employed on development of well at Clayton Cross, on baths at RUYAULCOURT & on TRESCAULT Water Point. 429 Fd Co on 22	[sgnd]
	24/28		427 Fd Co engaged in taking census of billets in support Bde Area, completion of RUYAULCOURT Baths and work on TRESCAULT and CLAYTON CROSS Water Points, also reconnoitres well in Bde forward Area. 428 Fd continued reconnaissance and gas proofing of dug-outs, making & lettering signboards for trenches &c in forward area. Dug-out strengthened at 126 Bde Nucleus Station. Reconnaissance made & traps removed during & after operation on 28th. 429 Fd Co on general improvements & work on water supply. 0827st Coy standing by, Notification of relief by NZ Div on night 28/29th. HQ RE did not change quarters.	[sgnd]
	29th and 30th		427 and 429 Field Coys moved to BERTINCOURT. 428 Fd Co remained in HAVRINCOURT WOOD and worked on baths at TRESCAULT also on fixing troughs at well at RIBECOURT. This water point of 42 Div Area but the unsatisfactory state of Mains at TRESCAULT necessitated application being made for permission to draw water from this point 427 Fd Co continued work on TRESCAULT and CLAYTON CROSS water points, installing a Power Chain Helix Pump at the latter. 429 Field Co worked on water supply, laying and assisting Bdes in provision of comfortable quarters for troops in rest.	[sgnd]

S E C R E T.

O.C. 427 Field Coy, R.E.
O.C. 428 Field Coy, R.E.
O.C. 429 Field Coy, R.E.
O.C. No: 1 Secn, 252 Tunn: Coy, R.E.
O.C. 1/7th North'd Fus: (P).

DISTRIBUTION OF WORK ON 'Z' DAY.

1. Each Field Company may detail eight Sappers to be attached to the Brigade to which they are affiliated for reconnaissance and repair of dugouts - These men will be attached to Brigade and Battalion Headquarters.
   During the ensuing operations, the distribution of the remainder of the Field Companies will be controlled from this office.

2. Work will commence four hours after ZERO on 'Z' day - 'Z' day and ZERO will be notified later.

3. (a) O.C. 428 Field Coy, R.E. will continue work on the TRESCAULT Well by day and by night; giving all possible assistance to 149 A.T. Coy, R.E., who are responsible for the erection of the pumping plant and all piping. (The engine and pump are being sent to TRESCAULT this evening.)
(b) At ZERO plus 240 minutes an Officers reconnaissance party will proceed to BEAUCAMP and report as speedily as possible on the condition of the Water Point.
(c) At ZERO plus 240 minutes a dugout reconnaissance party will report to 125th and 127th Brigade Headquarters respectively. These parties will be made up jointly by O.C. 428 Field Coy, R.E. and O.C. No: 1 Secn, 252 Tunnelling Coy, R.E. and will be organised in two detachments, a small party for reconnaissance and a second party for gas-proofing and minor repairs to dugouts. To assist in this work O.C. 1/7th North'd Fus: (P) will detail one platoon to report to Headquarters, 428 Field Coy, R.E. at ZERO plus 180 minutes. As there are likely to be more dugouts in the 127 Brigade Area, this party should be the stronger.
   Attention is drawn to instructions previously issued regarding the marking of dugouts.
(d) As soon as the situation permits O.C. 428 Field Coy, R.E. will arrange for an Officer to make a reconnaissance of the most suitable tracks running East and West and have same marked with pickets or tracing tapes as necessary.
   This officer will call at Brigade Headquarters on his way and obtain their views and instructions.

4. O.C. 427 Field Coy, R.E. will develop the Water Point (Q.8.a.0.45.) near CLAYTON'S CROSS, according to the yield of the well. This supply is intended primarily for Water Carts. A 2,300 gall: Storage Tank will be erected with the usual pumps and standards.
(b) He will complete the erection of and approaches to the 9,000 gall: Storage Tank ~~will be erected with the usual pumps and standards.~~ (to be fed by Garford lorries) in Q.15.a.
(c) As soon as the situation permits he will push on with the TRESCAULT Well Water Point (Q.10.a.4.6.) completing Storage Tank, Standards and Water Bottle Filler at the earliest possible moment and erecting 600 gall: Troughs. It is the intention to have at least 12 Troughs ultimately at this point, for which O.C. 149 A.T. Coy, R.E. will provide necessary wrought iron piping, valves, etc. to connect, to be gravity fed from the 9,000 gall: Storage Tank.
   To assist in the above work O.C. 427 Field Coy, R.E. may call upon two Platoons of 1/7th North'd Fus: (P) and two Tip Carts, rendezvous and times to be fixed by Os.C. concerned.

5.   O.C. 429 Field Coy, R.E. will detail one Section to stand by to load Pontoon and Trestle Equipment on three Field Companies bridging vehicles at Bridging Stores (I.21.b.9.7.)
The remainder of the Company will standby for orders.

6.   O.C. No: 1 Section, 252 Tunnelling Coy, R.E. will cease work on dugouts on 26th instant, and detail his men as laid down in para: (3) above.
He will also arrange for a rapid reconnaissance of the following roads for land mines, as soon as the situation allows :-

    TRESCAULT - RIBECOURT,
    TRESCAULT - BEAUCAMP,
    Roads running N. and S. across Divisional Front, as the move forward permits.

7.   O.C. 1/7th North'd Fus: (P) will take all necessary steps to keep open roads and tracks for which the Division is responsible. This should include a Mounted Officers patrol to ensure quick repairs as necessary.
He will also arrange for the immediate opening for double lorry traffic of the TRESCAULT - RIBECOURT, TRESCAULT - BEAUCAMP - VILLERS PLOUICH roads as the situation develops.

8.   Work in Hand. All work on accommodation, etc. (including D.H.Q. dugouts) will cease on 26th instant, so that every available man can be employed on 27th instant.
It is desirable that some men should be kept in hand by all units so that double shifts may be worked as necessary.

9.   R.E. Stores. An Advanced R.E. Dump has been established at RUYAULCOURT (P.10.c.3.8.) and a further small dump of wiring materials, mining sets, boarding and three Trench Bridges at Q.15.a.7.5. If the situation permits the stores at the later point will be brought forward to TRESCAULT Well Q.10.a.4.5. at which place a supply of anti-gas cloth, Tracing Tapes, and Wire Cutters will also be kept.

J.S. Riddich
Lieut: Colonel,
C.R.E., 42nd DIVISION.

26-9-18.

Copy to HQrs, 42nd Divn. 'G')
       H.Qrs, 125th Inf: Bde.)
       H.Qrs, 126th Inf: Bde.) For information.
       H.Qrs, 127th Inf: Bde.)
       O.C. 149 A.T. Coy, R.E.)

No 21

ORIGINAL

WAR DIARY.

Headquarters 42nd Divisional R.E.

October 1918

Copies & Ay
for CRE 142nd Division

Army Form C. 2118.

WAR DIARY
or
INTELLIGENCE SUMMARY.
(Erase heading not required.)

Instructions regarding War Diaries and Intelligence Summaries are contained in F.S. Regs., Part II. and the Staff Manual respectively. Title pages will be prepared in manuscript.

Place	Date	Hour	Summary of Events and Information	Remarks and references to Appendices
VELU	1/10/18		HQ RE (with 42nd DHQ) at VELU. 427 Field Co moved from BERTINCOURT to HAVRINCOURT WOOD, 428 Field Co in HAVRINCOURT WOOD, work on tracks at TRESCAULT. Reconnaissance of ESCAUT River & Canal. 429 Field Coy at BERTINCOURT working on water supply in RUYAULCOURT and METZ.	KWB
	2/10/18		428 Field Co made reconnaissance of wells in Villers Plouich and La Vacquerie engineer services for 126 Bde. Clearing down & filling pot holes on TRESCAULT-RIBECOURT Road & wells in RIBECOURT. 427 & 429 Fld Coys employed as yesterday. 429 Field Coy moved to TRESCAULT	KWB
	3/10/18		427 & 428 Field Coys a.a. on 2nd. 429 on erection of new Bwd WR.	KWB
	4/10/18		428 Field Co moved to TRESCAULT. Continued with repairs to TRESCAULT RIBECOURT Rd. & on wells in RIBECOURT. 427 & 429 Fld Coys employed as yesterday.	KWB
	5/10/18		All Coys continued with work in hand	KWB
	6/10/18		Personnel of Field Coys, who could be dispensed with in the carrying out of work already undertaken, engaged on learning	KWB
	7/10/18		on the 8' mat. HQ RE (with 42 DHQ) moved to TRESCAULT	KWB
	8/10/18			KWB
TRESCAULT ESNES	9/10/18		HQ RE (with 42 DHQ) moved to ESNES. All 3 Field Coys moved to LESDAINS	KWB
	10/10/18		427 commenced on construction of 2 heavy bridges over Torrent d'Esnes, 428 on Water Supply reconnaissance for Bridy traps in ESNES. 429 also reconnoitering for trolly traps mines &c	KWB
	11/10/18		427 Complete work on bridges & established a Water Point in LESDAIN, 428 Field Co. reconnoitering of Water Points & dismantling off bridges over the Escaut River & Canal. 429 also on the dismantling of these bridges	KWB
BEAUVOIS	12/10/18		HQ RE (with 42 DHQ) moved to BEAUVOIS. 427 Field Co moved to FRAYELLE, 428 K and 429th Field Co moved to JEUNE BOIS (IIIc) on CAMBRAI-LECATEAU Rd.	KWB
	13/10/18		427 Field Co RE preparing timber and bridging equipment for bridges over R. SELLE for operation on the 20th. 428 Field Co employed on water points at BEAUVOIS BRASSERIE and AULICOURT FARM. 429 on felling of craters in Quiecourt Area	KWB

Army Form C. 2118.

WAR DIARY
or
INTELLIGENCE SUMMARY.
(Erase heading not required.)

Instructions regarding War Diaries and Intelligence Summaries are contained in F. S. Regs., Part II. and the Staff Manual respectively. Title pages will be prepared in manuscript.

Place	Date	Hour	Summary of Events and Information	Remarks and references to Appendices
BEAUVOIS	14th to 19th		Coys carried on with work in hand. 427 Field Co had to erect in all 11 bridges across the SELLE, 2 of which were to be pontoon bridges for getting guns across. 428 Field Coy carried out reconnaissance of water supply in VIESLY. 429 on construction of shelters for Brigade Battle HQ.	
	20th		On night 19/20th. Bridges were completed by 427 Field Co. Thanks to [bridges constructed] notice boards fixed and lamps at bridge heads all in time for the advance early morning of 20th inst. 428 Field Co on water supply, sent 1 Section on Reconnaissance work E of R. SELLE. 429 Field Coy also sent reconnaissance parties forward.	
	21st to 22nd		427 Field Co sorting out Bridging equipment into dumps and then into mobile loads. 428 Field Co dismantling huts at BRIASTRE also made a reconnaissance of OLD CARDON MILL (E 2 c and d) and just E of SOLESMES. 429 employed on clearance of demolished Railway Bridge S of SOLESMES.	
	23rd		427 Field Co. moved to SOLESMES. 428 employed on the various Waterpoints. 429 Field Co. moved to SOLESMES; made a reconnaissance of bridge over BEARD BROOK, E of SOLESMES.	
	24th 25th to		Coys. carried on as on 21st and 22nd. all three Field Coys. training, with the exception of parties who were engaged on preparation of Ring for Divl Boxing Tournament, Band Contest Ground and grounds for Divl RE sports. 428 Field coys carried out some improvements to the Divl Reception Camp.	
	31st		HQ RE still at BEAUVOIS, 427-429 Field Coys at SOLESMES, and 428 Field Co at JEUNE BOIS	

H.Q. R.E. 42nd DIVISION

9/8 22

ORIGINAL

WAR DIARY

November.
~~December~~   1918

VOLUME IV

Strength 3 Officers (Includes M.O.)
          10 Other Ranks

Army Form C. 2118.

WAR DIARY
or
INTELLIGENCE SUMMARY.

(Erase heading not required.)

Instructions regarding War Diaries and Intelligence Summaries are contained in F. S. Regs., Part II. and the Staff Manual respectively. Title pages will be prepared in manuscript.

Place	Date	Hour	Summary of Events and Information	Remarks and references to Appendices
HAUTMONT	1/11/18		H.Q. R.E. (with 42nd DHQ) remain at BEAUVOIS. 427 & 429 Field Cos at SOLESMES. 428 Field Coy at BEAUVOIS. Divisional R.E. held sports on 1st inst. From 2nd to 4th instants Corps were employed on training. Parties engaged on improvements to Divl Theatre, preparation of grounds for Divisional Band Contest and Football Competition, also on completion of small details on trestle bridge at BRIASTRE.	10MR
	to 4/11/18			
POTELLE	5/11/18		On 5th inst. instructions were received for H.Q. R.E. (with DHQ) to move to BEAUDIGNIES. On arrival there & consequent upon further instructions, H.Q. R.E. (with D.H.Q.) moved to POTELLE. 429 Field Co. moved to LE CARNOY. 428 & 429 Field Cos. to LE QUESNOY.	10MR
	6/11/18		428 & 429 Field Coys moved to LE CARNOY. Field Corps made reconnaissance of roads through FORET DE MORMAL and repairs were carried out with a view to the carrying forward of bridging equipment in readiness for the bridging of the R. SAMBRE. 429 Weldon trestle bridge was put across craters at N.35.c.2.6, & a deviation made round craters at N.29 & 84. Work commenced on diversion bridge over blown culvert at N36.a.5.6.	10MR
	7/11/18		Companies engaged on bridging of craters in FORET DE MORMAL. During the day Companies moved to PETIT BAVAY.	10MR
PETIT BAVAY	8/11/18		H.Q. R.E. (with 42nd DHQ) moved to PETIT BAVAY. Early morning of 8th a light pontoon bridge was put across the R. SAMBRE and reconnoitring parties from 429 Field Co proceeded forward of the SAMBRE viâ forward Battns. Portion of 428 Field Co moved to HAUTMONT and portion of 429 Field Coy moved to BOUSSIERES.	10MR
HAUTMONT	9/11/18		H.Q. R.E. with (42nd DHQ) moved to HAUTMONT. 427 & 428 Field Coys concentrated in HAUTMONT and built a trestle bridge over the River SAMBRE. A heavy bridge over the SAMBRE was commenced. 429 Field Co. at BOUSSIERES, PETIT BAVAY and employed on road diversion.	10MR
	10/11/18		Footbridge constructed over debris of old HAUTMONT BRIDGE. 429 & 428 Coys were engaged on the Heavy bridge at HAUTMONT. Two sections of 429 Field Co moved FERRIERE LA GRANDE to commence work on light bridge over R. SOLRE.	10MR

Army Form C. 2118.

WAR DIARY
or
INTELLIGENCE SUMMARY.
(Erase heading not required.)

Instructions regarding War Diaries and Intelligence Summaries are contained in F. S. Regs., Part II. and the Staff Manual respectively. Title pages will be prepared in manuscript.

Place	Date	Hour	Summary of Events and Information	Remarks and references to Appendices
HAUTMONT	11/11/18		Official intimation received that armistice with Germany has been signed. Hostilities cease this day at 1100 hours 429 & 428 Field Coys still engaged on heavy bridge at HAUTMONT & in the execution of various Engineer services throughout Divisional Area. 429 Field Co moved other section to FERRIERE to work on bridge at FERRIERE LA GRANDE and FERRIERE LA PETITE. Three Coys carried on with work in hand. 429 Field Coy moved a portion of the Coy to HAUTMONT.	62MB
	11th & 12th			62MB
	13th			62MB
	14th		Heavy bridge over R. SAMBRE completed. 429 Field Coy completed bridge at Q.23.9.0.	62MB
	15th & 16th & 17th		Took over work on bridge at B.17.0.8.2 from 62 DIV. Completed on 16th. A bridge to take "A" Class loads was erected over R. SAMBRE at BOIS LE BOIS. 429 Field Co. concentrated at HAUTMONT on 14th. From this date to the end of the month, Coys were engaged on cleaning up &, as far as the carrying out of the necessary R.E. Services would allow, Various improvements were made at Divisional Theatre & at D.R.S. reshawls. Construction of Boxing Ring, destruction of German Explosives. Repairs effected to billets & improvements made on transport lines dismantling of pontoon bridge at BOUSSIERE, Heating apparatus at D.H.G. Div Theatre	62MB
	to 30th		During the latter half of the month slips were taken in connection with the Educational Scheme, and particulars taken in connection with the Scheme for Demobilisation. Lt J.E. ARKIESON, 427 Field Co R.E. appointed Divisional R.E. Education & Demobilisation Officer.	

R M Paterson
Capt.

ORIGINAL

WAR DIARY

of H.Q.rs 42nd Divl. R.E.

for month of

DECEMBER 1918

H.Q.,
42ND (E.L.) DIVISION,
R.E.
No.
Date. 4/1/1919

ORIGINAL

Army Form C. 2118.

WAR DIARY
INTELLIGENCE SUMMARY

Refce Maps:-
VALENCIENNES } 1:100,000
NAMUR

HEADQUARTERS 42nd DIVISIONAL R.E.

Place	Date	Hour	Summary of Events and Information	Remarks and references to Appendices
HAUTMONT	1-12-18 to 5-12-18		All three Field Coys. (including Transport lines) and H.Q. R.E. situated in HAUTMONT. 427 Fd. Coy. employed in completing heavy bridge at SOUS-LE-BOIS, fitting handrails and whitewashing same and wheelguards. On the 3rd inst. 427 Fd Cy dismantled Pontoon bridge at SOUS-LE-BOIS and transferred all equipment to Coys. Bdqrs. In addition a few small jobs were done by the Coys, otherwise they were engaged in Training during this period.	60/A
	6.12.18		Major M.S. HANMER (429 Fd Cy) with 1 complete section from each Coy, and 1 Platoon 1/10th A.V.R. (?) left HAUTMONT en route for CHARLEROI to prepare for the Division's occupation of that area. This advance party moved in 3 stages, 1 day to BINCHE, 2nd day to FONTAINE L'EVEQUE and 3rd day to CHARLEROI. 1 Section 428 Fd. Cy. R.E. and 3 Section 429 Fd Coy took Section transport and went to H.S. PAUL (429 Fd Cy) to VIEUX RENG to work on bridge, culverts etc.	60/A
	7.12.18 to		Remaining portions of Coys at HAUTMONT employed in cleaning vehicles and assisting on Transport lines owing to shortage of drivers. On 10th inst. 1 Section 428 Fd Coy moved by motor lorry to CHARLEROI coming under orders of Major HANMER.	
	12.12.18		1 Section 426 Fd Cy., 3 Section 429 Fd Cy. moved from VIEUX RENG area by motor lorry to CHARLEROI, having completed a bridge at VIEUX RENG and repaired a field in crater and culvert at ÉLESMES. 1 Section (428 Fd Cy) under orders of Major HANMER moved from CHARLEROI to FLEURUS.	60/A

WAR DIARY
INTELLIGENCE SUMMARY

Army Form C. 2118.

Place	Date	Hour	Summary of Events and Information	Remarks and references to Appendices
CHARLEROI	13-12-18		2 Section 427 Fd.Coy. proceeded to MARPENT to reconstruct medium Pontoon bridge - this was done on 14th inst. in 6 hours, total span 90'. HQ R.E. moved by motor lorry to CHARLEROI and opened an office in the ATHÉNÉE ROYAL. Coy (at HAUTMONT) preparing for forthcoming move (by march route)	B.M.
	14.12.18 to		Remainder of Coy. at HAUTMONT moved (under Brigade arrangements) by march route, marching each day except 17th inst. when they halted, and arrived at JESUIT COLLEGE, CHARLEROI, where billets were prepared by the Adj. RE (Capt W.H. BATEMAN) proceeded on	
	16.12.18		during the afternoon of the 18th. The Adj. RE (Capt W.H. BATEMAN) proceeded on short leave in France on 17th inst. D.H.Q. arrived in CHARLEROI and took over their quarters at 114 Boulevard AUDENT to which house HQRE. moved into on 18th inst.	B.M.
	19-12-18 to		Coy chiefly employed on improving quarters, billets etc. when (Division and working parties) forms, beds, cookhouses etc. 1 Section 408 Fd Coy. still	15M.B
	24.12.18		at FLEURUS on similar work for 127 Inf. Bde.	
	25.12.18 26.12.18		Two days holiday. Special dinners arranged each day, followed by dancing, concert, whist drives on both days.	15M.B
	27.12.18 to		The 428 Fd.Coy. commenced work in wiring in a Army Ration Dump at MONTIGNIES. 64th work on before continued. Work commenced on 31st on FOURTH ARMY Population	
	31.12.18		Signal Camp at JUMET. Beds etc. etc. installed. Major KITCHEN M.C. R.V.C. posted to 1/2(E.L) Field Ambce. and struck off strength HQ R.E. from 28.12.18.	15M.B

The Adjt. R.E. (Capt BATEMAN) Returned from Leave in FRANCE

Army Form C. 2118.

WAR DIARY
INTELLIGENCE SUMMARY.
(Erase heading not required).

Place	Date	Hour	Summary of Events and Information	Remarks and references to Appendices
CHARLEROI	31.12.18		CASUALTIES DURING MONTH :—	
			Capt. W.H. BATEMAN M.C. To Short leave in FRANCE 17.12.18	
			—do— Rejoined from —do— 30.12.18	
			Major H. THERRY M.O. R.A.M.C. posted to 1/2 (E.L) Fd Amb. 28.12.18 None.	
			(struck off strength of H.Q.R.E.)	
			1 OR (Sapr HERBERT) to 14 days leave in U.K.	
			2 OR (Hope PARKER and Dr JONES) rejoined from 14 days leave in U.K.	

Bateman
Captain R.E.
Actg. for C.R.E.
42ND (E. LANCS) DIV.

H.Q.
42ND (E.L) DIVISION.
R.E.
31.12.18

Vol 24

WAR DIARY
OF
H.Q. 2nd (E Lancs) Divisional R.E.
from Jan 1st to 31st, 1919
(Volume 6)

Army Form C. 2118.

WAR DIARY
or
INTELLIGENCE SUMMARY.

Ly Not BELGIUM
NAMUR sheet 5 1:100000

(Erase heading not required.)

Instructions regarding War Diaries and Intelligence Summaries are contained in F. S. Regs., Part II. and the Staff Manual respectively. Title pages will be prepared in manuscript.

Place	Date	Hour	Summary of Events and Information	Remarks and references to Appendices
CHARLEROI	1-1-19		———— HEADQUARTERS 42 DIVISIONAL R.E. ————	
			All three Field Coys. and H.Q.R.E. situated at CHARLEROI. The Field Coys. being billeted at the JESUIT COLLEGE. H.Q.R.E. situated at Boulevard AUDENT of D.H.Q. 427 F. Coy. on hutting for Div.l Rest Stn., Entraining roof for Aerial Service, Huts for 126 Brigade. General improvement of Billets & Coy. Transport Lines. Work on Concentration Camp at JUMET. 428 F. Coy. employed at JUMET making a building suitable for a Demob.n Concentration Camp. Swimming Baths at CHARLEROI, and at Div.l Baths, Disinfector, and Coy. Transport Lines. Minor services for D.H.Q. and R.A. also for 127 Inf. Brigade. 429 F. Coy. employed at Demob.n & Concentration Camp at JUMET. Working about the Cavalry, Infantry Barracks CHARLEROI, and at Div.l Baths, Disinfector & Company Transport Lines.	[initials]
	7-1-19			
	8-1-19		427 F. Coy. Continuation of works as above. Corps Commander expressed approval of work done by Coy. at JUMET. Work on Concent.n Camp at JUMET abandoned. Work at Huts for 125 Fd. A.S.C. commenced. 10th Ont. Lieut.t P.R. ROBINSON, R.E. and F.H. DART, R.E. struck off strength of Coy. for Demobilization. 428 F. Coy. Continuation of works as above, in addition, works on the Div.l Theatre and constructing a wire fence, round Ration Dump at MONTIGNIES. Billets of Men broken into on the 8th inst, and considerable Government property stolen, by persons unknown. 429 F. Coy. Continuation of works as above. Work at Concent.n Camp abandoned on the 9th inst. Lieut.t	[initials]
	to			
	11-1-19		J.F. NICOLSON, R.E. for demobilization on 9th inst.	
	12-1-19		All 3 companies. Church Parade. Horses & Mules closed for Demobilization.	[initials]

Army Form C. 2118.

WAR DIARY
or
INTELLIGENCE SUMMARY.

Ref. Maps _BELGIUM_

NAMUR. Sheet 8 1:100,000

Place	Date	Hour	Summary of Events and Information	Remarks and references to Appendices
CHARLEROI	13-1-19		427 F. Coy. Works in hand continued. Work commenced in hutting for 27th M.A.C. on 13th inst. One Recreation Hut 20 x 21 completed on 14th inst. Work commenced on one Dining Hall 60 x 36, Canteen, Bath house and two cook-houses on 14th inst. Work commenced on Div. A.S.C. Hosp. on 13 th inst. Completed 125 Bde A.S.C. Transport Stables. 428 F. Coy. Works in hand continued. Station at FLEURUS withdrawn except 1 N.C.O & 2 Men for work with the Laying Pole. on the 13 th inst. Lieut. J. TAYLER. R.E. transferred from 428 F. Coy to 429 F. Coy on 14 th inst. Unloading stage completed, and checking of Coy Equipt. commenced on the 15th inst. 429 F. Coy. Work in hand completed. A party of Sen.rs R.E. detailed to attend Div.l formentation of Medal Ribbons on the 17th inst. Recipients:- Lt. Col. RIDDICK. J.S. D.S.O. (H.Q.R.E.). Capt. BATEMAN. W.H. M.C. (H.Q.R.E.). Major J.S. ENTWISTLE. M.C. 428 Field Coy R.E. N°.418047 Serg.t B. TEMPLETON. M.M. N°. 217082. L/Cpl BUTLER. W.H. M.M. N°. 430347 Serg.t WILLIAMSON. M.M. N°. 442 410 Sapr. (A/2nd Corp.). ASHWORTH. N.M. 427 F. Coy. N°. 440312 Cpl. Scott J.M. Croix de Guerre (French) 428 F. Coy. 18° 442/47 Serg.t JOHNSON. T.H. M.M. 429 F. Coy.	cont.d
	15-1-19		427 F. Coy. Rest and Church Parade. 428 F. Coy. Work continued, assisted by Working parties from U.W.S. (Pierson) 429 F. Coy. Rest and Church Parade.	cont.d
	19-1-19			
	20-1-19		427 F. Coy. Works on hand continued. Div.l H.Q. Guard Room commenced nothing. Lieut W. L. MELLOR. R.E. Left Unit and reported to R.T.O. COLOGNE for duty with him on 21 st inst. Inspection of Coy. Billets and Transport Lines by C.R.E on the 22nd & 23rd inst. Completed D.H.Q Guard Room & Div.l Recept.n Camp 24th inst.	cont.d
			428 F. Coy. and 429 F. Coy. Works as above.	cont.d
	25-1-19			
	26-1-19		All companies - Rest and Church Parade.	

Army Form C. 2118.

WAR DIARY
or
INTELLIGENCE SUMMARY.
(Erase heading not required.)

Instructions regarding War Diaries and Intelligence Summaries are contained in F. S. Regs., Part II. and the Staff Manual respectively. Title pages will be prepared in manuscript.

REF MAP BELGIUM
NAMUR Sheet 5 1:100,000

Place	Date	Hour	Summary of Events and Information	Remarks and references to Appendices
CHARLEROI	29-1-19		Inspection of Coy Billets and Transport Lines by the Divisional Commander on 29th inst. 427 F. Coy. Works on hand continued. Commenced work on stabling for A.S.C. on 28th inst. Completed New Bearer Station on the 29th inst. 428 F. Coy. Works on hand continued. Work on Div: Theatre completed 27th inst. Bowing Ring erected at UNIVERSITÉ du TRAVAIL, CHARLEROI, on 27th inst. Minor services for Coy H.Q. & Transport Lines carried out. Bowing Ring dismantled, and placed in store for further use if required. 429 F. Coy. Works on Infantry Barracks. Repair work at R.E. Dump. A party inspected Bridges over SAMBRE in town, as it was alleged that the Germans had left a large quantity of explosives, in holes made in the abutment. Nothing was found.	15md [?] bxR [?]
	31-1-19		— Casualties during Month — I.O.R. (Sergt. S.W. Gould) arrived from Base 2-1-19 " " " Special Leave (14 days) to U.K. 10-1-19. " (Sergt. G. Herbert) struck off Strength. Demobilized 5-1-19. Capt. J.P. Eshlin from Base. attached to H.Q. R.E. from 427 F. Coy 9-1-19. I.O.R. (R.S.M. H.J. Jeuvray) returned from special leave 15-1-19	

B H Bateman
Adjutant Capt.
For C.R.E. 42nd Div.

Army Form C. 2118.

WAR DIARY
or
INTELLIGENCE SUMMARY.

(Erase heading not required.)

42ND DIVISIONAL R.E.

FEBRUARY 1919.

VOLUME.

Army Form C. 2118.

WAR DIARY
or
INTELLIGENCE SUMMARY.
(Erase heading not required.)

Instructions regarding War Diaries and Intelligence Summaries are contained in F. S. Regs., Part II. and the Staff Manual respectively. Title pages will be prepared in manuscript.

Place	Date	Hour	Summary of Events and Information	Remarks and references to Appendices
			HEADQUARTERS 42 DIVISIONAL R.E.	
CHARLEROI	1/2/19		All three Field Coys and Divl H.Q.R.E. situated at CHARLEROI and billeted at the Jesuit College. H.Q.R.E. situated at 114 Boulevard AUDENT at D.H.Q. 427 Field Coy. Work on stabling for A.S.C. General Barrack duties. Church parade on the 4th inst, and 10th inst. Church parade 9th inst. 428 Field Coy. Works on hand continued. Completed two Huts for "C" 211 Bat. R.F.A. on the MONTIGNIES-GILLY. R.D. Work on disinfector for "B" 211 Bde. at FLEURUS held up owing to severe weather. Commenced 60 x 20 Hut for IV Corps at MARCHIENNE, and two French Marquees for D.A.D.R.T. at CHARLEROI. 429 Field Coy. Works on hand continued. Repairs to vehicles. Hutting at HUNTIGNY. Brigade Workshops, Iny Barracks. Work on Divl Theatre 3rd inst.	
	12/2/19		427 Field Coy. Works on hand continued. Completed stables for A.S.C. & 1st Tent. Church parade 16th inst.	
	13/2/19		" " " Work on Transport Lines. Sketching Coy Equipt. 2nd Lieut LORD. REID.	
			428 " " " Proceeded to CONCENT as Draft conducting Otr on 15-2-19. Water cart damaged owing to an accident on the Rd and Commenced work on 6 platforms for Amtn at ONOZ, on the 20th inst. Coy reduced to Cadre B" on 21st inst. Works at D.H.Q on 22nd inst. Work at CHARLEROI station completed 23rd inst.	
			429 Field Coy. Works on hand continued. Sketching Coy Stores. General Barrack duties. D.H.Q R.E 533 F Coy 3 all turned out to assist in putting out Fire which broke out at D.H.Q on the 19th inst.	
	23/2/19		427 Field Coy. Works on hand continued. Completed French Marquees. Mobilization Equipt stored at CHARLEROI Barracks. Vehicles parked at Divl Park 16th inst.	
	24/2/19		428. Field Coy. Works on hand continued. Mobilization Equipt stored at CHARLEROI Barracks. Vehicles parked at Divl Park, and receipts obtained. Instructions received for all Units to be prepared to drop to Cadre A on short notice.	
	28/2/19		429 Field Coy. Works on hand continued. Mobilization Equipt stored at CHARLEROI Barracks. H.Q R.E vehicle parked with 429 Field Coy vehicles and vehicles parked at Div Park.	

WAR DIARY
or
INTELLIGENCE SUMMARY.

Divisional H.Q. R.E. (Casualties)

Capt. J. P. Echlin M.C. R.E. joined H.Q.R.E 16-2-19
" Lt. W. H. Bateman — " — Left H.Q.R.E for U.K. 17-2-19.
" J. P. Echlin — " — " for Leave to U.K. 18-2-19
" " — " — rejoined from Leave 26-2-19
2/Corp. Horsfield ⎫
" Parker ⎬ Left for Concentration Camp (Demobⁿ) 22-2-19.
Driv. Mason ⎪
" Laidlaw ⎪
" Collins ⎭

Sap. Blackmore 427 L. Coy R.E. ⎫
" Colman 428 " " " ⎬ Transferred to H.Q.R.E. 23-2-19.
" Robinson 428 " " " ⎭

Army Form C. 2118.

WAR DIARY
or
INTELLIGENCE SUMMARY.
(Erase heading not required.)

Vol 26

WAR DIARY.

H.Q. R.E. 42nd Division.
from 1st to 31st March. 1919.

(Volume 5)

H.Q.
42ND (E.L.) DIVISION.
R.E.

WAR DIARY
or
INTELLIGENCE SUMMARY.
(Erase heading not required.)

Army Form C. 2118.

H.Q.
42ND (E.L.) DIVISION.
R.E.

Instructions regarding War Diaries and Intelligence Summaries are contained in F. S. Regs., Part II. and the Staff Manual respectively. Title pages will be prepared in manuscript.

Place	Date	Hour	Summary of Events and Information	Remarks and references to Appendices
Charleroi	1/3/19 to 18/3/19		During the month the Divisional R.E. have been demobilized down to Cadre A.	
			All stores have been checked + packed in accordance with Demobilization Instructions.	J.E.
			All vehicles have been stripped + parked on the Champ Des Manoeuvres ready for entrainment.	
			Some work was done at the Rest Camp, Charleroi Main Station + also at the News Church Fromet Hut in Charleroi.	
	19/3/19 to 31/3/19		Lt. Col. J.G. Riddick DSO RE. CRE. 42nd Divn went on leave to U.K. (Orders were received that the Division will proceed to OSWESTRY (Via ANTWERP + IMMINGHAM) + hand over stores here, and be demobilized.	J.E.
			A.29 Field Coy RE left Charleroi for Antwerp " on 2nd April 1919.	
			428 " " " " " " on 3rd April 1919.	
			427 " " + HQ RE will leave Charleroi for Antwerp on 3rd April 1919.	
			Casualties of HQ RE caused by Demobilization have been made up by transferring Sapper Blackmore + Colman from 427 Field Coy + Sapper Robinson from A29 F.C. R.E. 42 Divn.	J.E. CRE 42 Divn

1/4/19.

www.ingramcontent.com/pod-product-compliance
Lightning Source LLC
Chambersburg PA
CBHW081237170426
43191CB00034B/1789